BANDOBAST AND KHABAR

BANDOBAST AND KHABAR

REMINISCENCES OF INDIA

COLONEL CUTHBERT LARKING

GYAN

Published by

Gyan Publishing House
5, Ansari Road
Daryaganj, New Delhi-110002
Phone: 011-47034999, 9811692060
E-mail: books@gyanbooks.com

Distribution Network
gyanbooks.com
India, USA, Canada, UK, Australia, France

ISBN: 978-81-212-8925-2 (PB)
First Published, 1888

2nd Impression 2023

Printed at: Gyan Press, Delhi.

BANDOBAST AND KHABAR

AUTHOR: COLONEL CUTHBERT LARKING

BANDOBAST AND KHABAR.

THE NAWAB'S BIG TIGER

BANDOBAST AND KHABAR

REMINISCENCES OF INDIA

BY

COLONEL CUTHBERT LARKING

Illustrated

FROM ORIGINAL DRAWINGS BY THE AUTHOR

LONDON:
HURST AND BLACKETT, LIMITED,
13, GREAT MARLBOROUGH STREET.
1888.

I dedicate this Book

TO

THE NAWÁB IKBÁL-UD-DOWLAH

VIKÁR-UL-UMRA,

OF HYDERABAD,

THROUGH WHOSE GENEROUS HOSPITALITY

I ENJOYED SEVEN WEEKS' BIG GAME SHOOTING

IN THE DECCAN JUNGLES.

C. L.

PREFACE.

In presenting these pages to the public, I do not wish it to be imagined for one moment that I pretend to give any fresh information about the people, customs and sport of India, well known as they are, and so often described by abler pens than mine.

My book is simply the record of a very pleasant time passed in the country, and if it induces others in the slightest degree to follow in my footsteps, they will, I am sure, not regret the time and money spent in the journey. For my own part, I cannot better express my feelings towards India than by saying, that I am impatiently looking forward to the day when I may revisit it, and the many friends I feel I have left there.

During one part of my travels I was regarded as in an official capacity, and although I saw many things of great interest and thoroughly enjoyed that part of my tour, yet as at the time I was not travelling independently, I have thought it best for that reason to entirely omit it from my book, lest my views and opinions might be thought to reflect those, however indirectly, of the personages with whom I had the honour of being associated.

CUTHBERT LARKING.

LAYSTON HOUSE, BUNTINGFORD,
December, 1887.

CONTENTS.

CHAPTER I.

CHAPTER II.

CHAPTER III.

CHAPTER IV.

CHAPTER V.

CHAPTER VI.

CHAPTER VII.

CHAPTER VIII.

CHAPTER IX.

CHAPTER X.

CHAPTER XI.

CHAPTER XII.

CHAPTER XIII.

CHAPTER XIV.

ILLUSTRATIONS.

CHAPTER I.

I AM INVITED TO STAY WITH THE DUKE AND DUCHESS OF CONNAUGHT IN INDIA—I LEAVE LONDON—MY TRAVELLING COMPANION, COLONEL ARTHUR PAGET—STORM—GIBRALTAR—ROYAL YACHT 'OSBORNE'—MALTA—CURIOUS COINCIDENCE—PORT SAID—ITS AMENITIES—OPENING OF SUEZ CANAL—ADEN—A CONTEST OF OPINION—ARRIVE AT BOMBAY.

CHAPTER I.

His Royal Highness the Duke of Connaught was appointed to the command of the Rawul Pindi division of the Indian army during the summer of 1886, and, with the Duchess, sailed for India, to take up his command in the beginning of September. Before their departure, and whilst I was staying with them at Bagshot, I had expressed my great wish to see India, and they kindly invited me to go out and pay them a visit. This opportunity of seeing the country, I felt, was not to be missed, for I should probably witness scenes and phases of Indian life which do not fall to the lot of the ordinary tourist, and in this I was not disappointed.

The Colonial Exhibition in London had inspired many with a desire to see the great dependencies of the empire; but the Indian courts, with the natives at work, the gorgeous embroideries, silver, gold, and brass-work, and the picturesque arrangement of the whole section, seemed to attract more attention and interest than all the rest, so that, towards the end of the summer, every second person one met talked of going to India, and every available passage was taken in the Peninsular and Oriental steamers for months beforehand.

Colonel Arthur Paget and I had agreed to travel out together. I was anxious for as much sea-air as possible, and decided to go round by the Bay of Biscay; but as he preferred the shortest route, wishing to do duty with his regiment to the last, we agreed to meet at Port Said, he sailing by way of Brindisi. I took my passage on board the Peninsular and Oriental steamer *Mirzapore*, which, however, being bound for Calcutta, I arranged to leave at Port Said, and from thence to continue my journey in the steamer

Assam, belonging to the same company, and in which I should meet Paget.

I left London on the morning of the 4th of November, and joined the ship at Tilbury. There were crowds of passengers of all sorts—nuns, missionaries, young men about to join the Civil Service in India, older men returning from leave, newly-married couples, officers of the Army and Navy, and, in fact, members of every known profession. Amongst all this gathering I was glad to see Mr. Robert and Lady Susan Bourke (now Lord and Lady Connemara), he being on his way to take over the governorship of Madras. He was also accompanied by Lord Marsham, Mr. Rees, and Mr. Wingfield, members of his staff. Besides these, I had other friends in Mr. and Mrs. Gerard Leigh, Mr. Gordon, and Lord Gilford, &c.; so that altogether we formed a very cheery party, and agreed to dine at the same table.

The weather, which was fine at starting, underwent a great change during the night, when it came on to blow a gale, and the glass fell so rapidly that Captain Harvey determined to put in to Portland Harbour, and to remain there till the worst was over. There we stayed for thirty hours, the wind blowing a perfect hurricane, and the rain pouring in torrents, whilst the temperature was bitterly cold. Never shall I forget the misery of those hours. No one had had time to settle down, and many were regretting their friends and relations, with whom, they felt, they might have spent another day. Although in harbour, we were some miles from land, and there was a heavy swell on, so that no one could get on shore. Altogether, it was a wretched time, and I was very glad when, the gale having moderated a little, the captain decided to go out of harbour, and proceed with the journey.

The sea outside was running mountains high, and we had a very rough time of it, twice shipping green seas through the saloon skylight. But we finally reached Gibraltar at two p.m. on the 10th.

As soon as our ship stopped, I saw the steam-cutter of the *Osborne* come alongside, and I was carried off in her to the yacht, where we had a gathering of old friends. The *Osborne* was in dock, coaling, and undergoing some slight repairs. She had suffered in, and was much knocked about by, the late gales whilst taking Her Royal Highness the Duchess of Edinburgh from Marseilles to Malta, and was now minus her crown; her bowsprit having been also carried away.

I went on to Government House, the old convent, and called on Sir Arthur Hardinge, who, it turned out, had sent me off an invitation to lunch, but my friends in the *Osborne* had been so quick that they had carried me off before it arrived. He had just received the news of the Duke of Connaught's appointment to the command of the Bombay army, and it was here also that I heard the sad account of poor Archer the jockey's death.

As we had to sail off again at half-past five, we had not much time to enjoy the luxury of *terra firma* after our long tossing, and the time for leaving came all too soon, especially as here at

Gibraltar we dropped some of our friends, who had come out to join their yacht. Fortunately, the weather was now fine, and, with the Bay of Biscay behind us, we felt that the disagreeable part of the journey was over, and everyone seemed to rise to the fact that something should be done to pass the time pleasantly. Passengers who had not hitherto been seen appeared on deck, whilst sports and concerts were organised, and lotteries on the day's run were drawn each morning. The thermometer now registering seventy-two degrees, and the sea being calm, the journey was pleasant enough, and we reached Malta at eleven p.m. on November 13th. It was too late to go ashore with any comfort, and, as the coaling was not to begin till half-past five in the morning, I determined to turn in till then, when all deck cabins were to be locked up, to keep out the dirt and dust.

I passed a pleasant day in Malta, where I found many friends, both in the Army and in the Fleet. Their Royal Highnesses the Duke and

Duchess of Edinburgh very kindly asked two or three of us to lunch at St. Antonio, and Prince George of Wales was also there, serving as a lieutenant in the *Dreadnought.* The gardens of St. Antonio are a mass of orange-trees, which, at that time, were laden with fruit ripening, and presented a very pleasant and gay aspect to me, coming straight from the cold and fogs of England.

We left Malta the same evening at five, taking Captain and Lady Eva Quin on board, *en route* to Madras, as he is one of Mr. Bourke's aides-de-camp.

It was a curious coincidence that we arrived at Port Said on November 17th, the day of the year on which the Canal was opened in 1869. I was present on that occasion, and was one of the first to go through it. What a grand sight it was! The Empress of the French, then in the height of her glory, the Emperor of Austria, the Crown Prince of Prussia, and many minor potentates, all meeting in friendship to witness one of the wonders of modern civilization; and yet, but one short year afterwards, these same people were plunged in deadly warfare, the poor Empress an exile in a foreign country, and her husband a prisoner in Germany.

Port Said has grown immensely since those days, and is increasing in size and prosperity every year. If it had but a railway to Ismalia, to give it direct land communication with Cairo, it would soon eclipse Alexandria. Owners of property in the latter town make every opposition possible to this railway, but it is bound to come in time.

Port Said boasts of a *café chantant* and casino called 'The Eldorado,' with an orchestra composed of Hungarian women, and a roulette-table with twenty-four numbers and two zeros. As soon as a passenger-ship arrives in port, the orchestra tunes up and the tables are in full swing. It is said that the troop-ships alone are worth four thousand a-year to this establishment.

Mr. Royle, the Peninsular and Oriental agent

at Port Said, and his wife, have a most charming house here, which they built themselves and have furnished in excellent taste and with every luxury. Here they entertained me whilst I was waiting for the *Assam* to come into port, and they made my visit very pleasant. It was such a comfort to find oneself once more in an English house, with a big bed to sleep in, after being boxed up for a fortnight in a little cabin on board ship.

The *Assam* arrived at 3.30 p.m. on the 18th, and I got my things together and put them on board, as we sailed that evening, using the electric light to go through the Canal. I was sorry to lose my fellow-passengers in the *Mirzapore*, where we had been so cheery, but found others on the *Assam* in Lord Fife, Mr. Newton Ogle, and Colonel Paget. The *Assam* is a comfortable ship, but small, and on this journey was very full, so that whereas on the *Mirzapore* I had a deck cabin to myself, now I was relegated to a cabin below with two other passengers; not very pleasant, especially in hot weather. In the Red Sea it was dreadfully hot, although most days we had a nice head wind to keep us comfortable, and I had my bedding brought up every night and slept on deck. The worst of this arrangement is that it entails getting up at five o'clock in the morning, when they begin to scrub the decks, and we used to turn out as reluctantly as a parcel of school-boys on being called, and refresh ourselves with those vile decoctions which the Peninsular and Oriental Company are pleased to call tea and coffee.

We reached Aden at twenty-two minutes and a half past eleven o'clock on the morning of the 24th. The reason I give the time so minutely is, that a lottery was got up on board as to the hour at which we should cast anchor, the time to be decided by the captain's watch. Now, when the time was announced, there were two claimants for the prize, namely the passenger who had drawn number twenty-two and the owner of number twenty-three. There was a great difference of opinions as to who was entitled to it; all the passengers were canvassed for their opinions, but I forget how it was decided.

No sooner were we in port than the ship was surrounded by numbers of black Somali boys in canoes, who made a fearful noise clamouring for the passengers to throw them coins, for which they dived. As the place is infested with sharks, this would seem highly dangerous work, but they did not appear to mind, although one poor boy is minus a leg, it having been snapped off by one of these voracious monsters a year or two back. As a rule, I believe sharks rarely touch blacks, though very fond of white men, and I was told that quite recently one of the telegraph clerks who had gone out to bathe was never seen again, the supposition being that he was taken by sharks.

General Hogg, the governor of Aden, was away on leave, and Colonel Gossett, commanding the 54th Regiment, was acting in his place. He kindly asked us—*i.e.*, Fife, Paget, Ogle, and myself—to lunch at Government House, and afterwards took us over the fortifications, which are in course of construction. The new fort will, when completed and armed, be a most formidable work; it thoroughly commands all the approaches to Aden.

This must be an awful place to remain in for any length of time; not a tree, not a shrub or blade of grass to be seen. It looks a veritable desolation of desolations.

A regiment is always sent here for a year on its way home from service in India, and the gallant 54th seemed very glad that their year was nearly at an end, and that they would soon be home. I am sure that this thought has a good deal to do with the officers and men keeping up their health and spirits when one day passes like another, without the slightest relaxation or amusement.

All meat has to be brought one hundred and sixty miles from the African coast, and there are no fruit and vegetables except what can be procured from passing ships. Fresh water is all made in huge condensers, as the rainfall is too

EVENING ON THE INDIAN OCEAN

small to be calculated upon for a regular supply.

We were none of us sorry to leave Aden and to find ourselves in the Indian Ocean, which was many degrees cooler than the Red Sea, and we congratulated ourselves that the back of our journey was broken, and that the next time we landed would be at Bombay.

The next six days were spent much as usual, in sports, reading, drawing, and watching the flying fish as they darted through the air alongside the ship. At last, on the evening of the 30th of November, we came in sight of the lights on the high tower at Bombay, and were soon anchored off the Apollo Bunda.

CHAPTER II.

FIRST IMPRESSIONS OF THE EAST—A MOTLEY CROWD—PARSEES, HINDOOS, AGENTS, ETC.—BYCULLA CLUB—ITS SPECIALITIES—GOVERNMENT HOUSE—ENORMOUS POPULATION—ELEPHANTA—FUNERAL PROCESSION—FUNERAL CEREMONIES OF PARSEES—THE NUMBER OF PARSEES—THEIR MORALITY AND RELIGION—TOWERS OF SILENCE DESCRIBED—ADVANTAGES AND DISADVANTAGES OF THE SYSTEM.

CHAPTER II.

Who can ever forget their first sight of the Oriental world?. Its glorious colouring, its strange faces and still stranger guttural tongues. It is like being suddenly transported into a different sphere, and wherever it may be—whether in Algiers, Tunis, Alexandria, Port Said, or any of the many ports on the southern shores of the Mediterranean—the feeling of intense novelty and admiration for the picturesque scene must be the same.

I, who have spent some years of my early youth in the East, cannot, of course, recall in myself the feelings and look of astonishment I have frequently seen on the faces of my fellow-passengers at their first introduction to an Oriental town, but still

I no less enjoy the picture, and am always glad to return and gaze on it.

Of the many places I have seen in the East, none has ever impressed me so much as Bombay on my first drive through it. I arrived there after sundown on the evening of the 30th of November. As soon as the ship was stopped, it was surrounded with innumerable shore-boats and hundreds of natives in different costumes or with no costumes at all. They scrambled up the sides in all directions, and seemed to take entire possession of the ship and passengers. There were Parsees busy trying to get hold of any gold the passengers might have in exchange for rupees or notes; touts from hotels; boys (as the native servants are called) showing their 'chits' and trying to get engaged on the spot; agents anxious to pass luggage through the custom-house; boatmen plying for hire; and a heap more, either on business or pleasure bent.

Lieutenant-Colonel Arthur Paget and I were travelling together, and we were met by a kind friend who had given up his dinner to come and take us ashore, and had made all arrangements for our comfort. He had engaged two boys for us, and our luggage was soon on board a private steam-launch, and we steamed off to the Apollo Bunda, that best known of all landing-places in the southern world. We had been made honorary members of the Byculla club, and bed-rooms had been engaged for us. Our friend had his carriage ready, and we drove off at once.

The Byculla club is about three miles from the landing-stage, and the road lies right through the native town and bazaars. Never shall I forget the sight. It was like a glimpse of the 'Arabian Nights.' The streets were crowded with natives, the shops illuminated with hundreds of little oil lamps. All kinds of strange-looking fruit and vegetables were being sold, and the brilliant colours, the dusky forms, the babble and gesticulations completed the picture.

One of the things that must impress the

stranger in India is the enormous population. The streets and houses seem always crowded, and it is the same wherever one goes. In travelling by rail, a large crowd is always to be seen at every station, all waiting for their turn, and that in the most patient and orderly manner. They each carry a small bundle, and a brass 'lota' for water, and are contented to be packed like sardines and locked up for hours together.

The Byculla club is a fine building, surrounded by lovely gardens, and built in one of the suburbs of Bombay. The members are most hospitable, and admit strangers, proposed and seconded by two members who are acquainted with them, to all the privileges of the club; and when I add that of all the clubs I was ever in, whether in England or the Continent, the Byculla is second to none in every comfort, I think it will be admitted that I am saying a good deal. We were shown two comfortable bed-rooms, with bath-room attached to each, as is, indeed, the case everywhere in India. As it was very sultry, our beds were put out on the balcony, with thick nets over them to keep out the mosquitoes.

We were awakened early in the morning by the noise made by the crows and mynahs, of which there seemed to be an innumerable quantity, and soon after our 'boys' brought us 'chota hazri' of tea, biscuits, and plantains.

I am very fond of the sensation of awaking in a strange place, and am always in a hurry to explore fresh ground, and on this occasion I dressed as soon as possible and went down. The rooms at the Byculla are large and lofty and the windows all open to the ground, so that there is always a delicious breeze through them. The gardens were ablaze with poincettias, red and yellow, and a mass of different kinds of crotons growing like laurels in England, whilst close to the front entrance stands a magnificent cocoa-palm; but, lovely as all this was, the sight of our breakfast appealed still more to our feelings. A broiled pomfret and a Byculla prawn curry are things to live for, and are themselves worth all the journey to Bombay. The first is a delicious flat fish, more delicate than anything I have ever tasted, the nearest approach I can make being that it seems like a cross between a flounder and a brook-trout. I believe it is only to be found near Bombay, and, though there it is plentiful enough, it is ever esteemed a great delicacy. With these two dishes, some small iced tomatoes, the size of grapes, and winding up with some of those delicious, loose-jacketed Indian oranges, we felt as if all the world went smoothly with us.

It was very hot, and regular Indians do not think of going out in the middle of the day, unless obliged to do so; but we were anxious to see all we could and as soon as possible, so, ordering a carriage, we drove off through Bombay to Government House at Malabar Point. It is a lovely drive, the road passing through groves of cocoa-nut palms and banana-trees, and gradually winding up-hill between villas and gardens, with the sea lying below like a huge lake, and covered with picturesque fishing-boats.

PARSEE TOWERS OF SILENCE BOMBAY

But why should I describe places and scenes of which volume after volume has been written? Who has not read about the Caves of Elephanta? and, if they have not, they will find them and other sights far better described in Arnold's 'India Re-visited' than my feeble pen can portray; so, with one exception, I will pass them all over, but the one exception interested me so much that I cannot refrain from writing about it. I refer to the Towers of Silence, or burial-place of the Parsees. I had heard a great deal about it, and had long been anxious to see it. On inquiry I found that an order had to be obtained from the secretary; so, calling at his office, I was most kindly received by Mr. Nusserwanjee Byramjee, who said he would meet us at the compound gateway at four o'clock, and show me over and explain everything I wished to know. We arrived there at the hour named, and were quite charmed with the beautiful view of Bombay and the harbour. The towers stand in a large garden or compound at the top of Malabar Hill, and the view of the town and sea is obtained over what seems a dense forest of cocoa-nut palms, though in reality this large grove is full of native houses and life. A funeral procession passed in whilst we were looking at the view, so that we had an opportunity of seeing the whole ceremony; but I think that, instead of using language of my own, I cannot do better than copy the admirable description of the Parsee religion and of the whole death-rites as written by Professor Monier Williams, and published in the *Times* of January 28, 1876; which description Mr. Byramjee gave me to read. Mr. Williams says:

'Your readers are doubtless aware that the Parsees are descendants of the ancient Persians, who were expelled from Persia by the Mahomedan conquerors, and who first settled at Surat about eleven hundred years ago. According to the last census, they do not number more than seventy thousand souls, of whom about fifty thousand are found in the city of Bombay and the remaining twenty thousand in different parts of India, but chiefly in Guzerat and the Bombay presidency. Though a mere drop in the ocean of two hundred and forty million inhabitants, they form a most important and influential body of men, emulating Europeans in energy and enterprise, rivalling them in opulence, and imitating them in many of their habits. Their vernacular language is Guzerathi, but nearly every adult speaks English with fluency, and English is now taught in all their schools. Their religion, as delivered in its original purity by their prophet Zoroaster, and as propounded in the Zend-Avesta, is monotheistic, or perhaps rather pantheistic, in spite of its philosophical dualism, and in spite of the apparent worship of fire and the elements, regarded as visible representations of the Deity. Its morality is summed up in three precepts of two words each: good thoughts, good words, good deeds; of which the Parsee is constantly reminded by the triple coil of his white woollen girdle. In its origin the Parsee system is allied to that of the Hindu Aryans—as represented in the Veda—and has much in common with the more recent Brahmanism. Neither religion can make any proselytes. A man must be born a Brahman or a Parsee; no power can convert him into either one or the other. One notable peculiarity, however, distinguishes Parseeism, nothing similar to its funeral rites prevails amongst other nations.

'The dakhmas, or Parsee towers of silence, are erected in a garden, on the highest point of Malabar Hill. The garden is approached by a private road, all access to which, except to Parsees, is barred by strong iron gates. The courteous secretary of the Parsee Punchayet, Mr. Nusserwanjee Byramjee, awaited my arrival at the entrance to the garden. He took me at once to the highest point in the consecrated ground, and we stood together on the terrace of the largest of the three Sagris, or houses of prayer, which overlook the five towers of silence. The principal Sagri contains the sacred fire, which when once kindled and consecrated by solemn ceremonial, is fed day and night with incense and fragrant sandal, and never extinguished.

'Beneath lay the city of Bombay, partially hidden by cocoa-nut groves, with its beautiful bay and harbour glittering in the brilliant December light. Beyond stretched the magnificent ranges of the ghauts, while immediately around us extended a garden such as can only be seen in tropical countries. No English nobleman's garden could be better kept, and no pen could do justice to the glories of its flowering shrubs, cypresses, and palms. It seemed the very ideal, not only of a place of sacred silence, but of peaceful rest.

'But what are those five circular structures which appear at intervals rising mysteriously out of the foliage? They are simply masses of masonry, massive enough to last for centuries, built of the hardest black granite, and covered with white chunam. Towers they scarcely deserve to be called, for the height of each is quite out of proportion to the diameter. The largest of the five, built with such solid granite that the cost of erection was three lakhs of rupees, seemed about ninety feet in diameter and not more than twenty-five feet in height. The oldest and smallest of the five was constructed two hundred years ago, when the Parsees first settled in Bombay, and is now only used by the Modi family, whose forefathers built it, and here the bones of many kindred generations are commingled. The next oldest was erected in 1756, and the other three during the succeeding century. A sixth tower stands quite apart from the others. It is square in shape and only used for persons who have suffered death for heinous crimes. The bones of convicted criminals are never allowed to mingle with those of the rest of the community.

'But the strangest feature in these strange, unsightly structures, so incongruously intermixed with graceful cypresses and palms, exquisite shrubs and gorgeous flowers, remains to be described.

'Though wholly destitute of ornament, and

even of the simplest moulding, the parapet of each tower possesses an extraordinary coping, which instantly attracts and fascinates the gaze. It is a coping formed, not of dead stone, but of living vultures. These birds, on the occasion of my visit, had settled themselves side by side in perfect order, and in a complete circle, around the parapets of the towers, with their heads pointed inwards; and so lazily did they sit there, and so motionless was their whole mien, that, except for their colour, they might have been carved out of the stone-work. After the towers have been once consecrated, no one except the corpse-bearers is allowed to enter, nor is any-one, not even a Parsee high-priest, permitted to approach within thirty feet of the immediate precincts. An exact model of the interior was, however, shown to me.

'Imagine a round column, or massive cylinder, twelve or fourteen feet high, and at least ninety feet in diameter, built throughout of solid stone, except in the centre, where a well, fifteen feet deep and forty-five feet in diameter, leads down to an excavation under the masonry, containing four drains at right angles to each other, terminated by holes filled with charcoal. Round the upper surface of this solid circular cylinder, and completely hiding the interior from view, is a stone parapet fourteen feet in height. The upper surface of the solid stone column is divided into seventy-two compartments, or open receptacles, radiating like the spokes of a wheel from the central well, and arranged in three concentric rings, separated from each other by narrow ridges of stone, which are grooved to act as channels for conveying all moisture from the receptacles into the well and into the lower drains.

'It should be noted that the number 3 is emblematical of Zoroaster's three precepts, and the number 72 of the chapters of his Yasna—a portion of the Zend-Avesta.

'Each circle of open stone coffins is divided from the next by a pathway, so that there are three circular pathways. In the outermost circle are placed the bodies of males, in the middle those of females, and in the inner and smallest circle, nearest the well, those of children.

'While I was engaged with the secretary in examining the model, a sudden stir amongst the vultures made us raise our heads. At least one hundred birds collected round one of the towers began to show symptoms of excitement, whilst others swooped down from neighbouring trees. The cause of this sudden abandonment of their previous apathy soon revealed itself. A funeral was approaching.

'However distant the house of a deceased person, and whether he be rich or poor, high or low rank, his body is always carried to the towers by the official corpse-bearers, called Nasasalar, who form a distinct class, the mourners walking behind. As the bearers are supposed to contract impurity in the discharge of their duty, they are forced to live quite apart from the rest of the community, and are therefore highly paid.

'The body, swathed in a white sheet, is placed

on a curved metal trough, open at both ends, and the corpse-bearers, dressed in pure white garments, proceed with it to the towers. They are followed by the mourners at a distance of at least thirty feet in pairs, also dressed in white, and each couple joined by holding a white handkerchief between them. When the two corpse-bearers reach the path leading by a steep incline to the door of the tower, the mourners turned back and entered the prayer-houses. The bearers carried the body into the tower, passing through the side door, and laid it, uncovered, in one of the open stone receptacles. In about five minutes they reappeared, with the empty bier and white cloth, and scarcely had they closed the door when a dozen vultures swooped down upon the body, and were rapidly followed by others. In five minutes more we saw the satiated birds fly back, and lazily settle down again on the parapet. Soon nothing is left but a skeleton. Meanwhile, the bearers are seen to enter a building shaped like a huge barrel. Then they changed their clothes, and washed themselves. Shortly afterwards we saw them come out and deposit their cast-off funeral garments on a stone receptacle near at hand. Not a thread leaves the garden lest it should carry deplement into the city. Perfectly new garments are supplied for each funeral.

'In a fortnight the same bearers return, and with gloved hands and implements resembling tongs, place the dry skeleton in the central well.'

I have copied out this long extract from Mr. Monier Williams' account, as it so exactly describes what I saw myself. There is a great deal to be said both for and against the system. It is excellent from a sanitary point, but I think it is most revolting to think of our dear dead exposed naked by a set of corpse-bearers and devoured by vultures. Stories are told of people living in houses in the neighbourhood who have sometimes found fingers or other parts of a human body on their verandah, carried there and dropped by these vultures. I may add that a Parsee believes

D 2

that if the right eye is plucked out first by the birds the soul goes to heaven, but if the left eye is taken first it goes to hell, the consequence being that on the amount received by the corpse-bearers depends a good deal the place where the soul of the deceased is supposed to go.

CHAPTER III.

MALABAR POINT—LEAVE BOMBAY FOR POONA—INDIAN RAILWAYS—GHAUTS—CLUB AT POONA—BAZAAR AND KINKOB WORK—LEAVE FOR HYDERABAD—JOURNEY—BIRDS ON TELEGRAPH WIRES—SCENERY NEAR HYDERABAD—RESIDENCY AT CHUDDERGHAUT—CITY OF HYDERABAD—DINE WITH THE NAWAB VIKAR UL UMRA—ARRANGE BIG-GAME SHOOTING—ATTAR OF ROSES—MEER ALUM TANK—TOMBS OF GOLCONDA—DIAMONDS NOT FOUND THERE—AFRICAN CAVALRY—LUNCH WITH THE NIZAM—NAWAB SAID HUSSEIN—NAUTCH DANCE—BLACK-BUCK HUNTING WITH CHEETAH—LUNCH WITH VIKAR UL UMRA—RETURN TO POONA—BOMBAY—DELHI—DAK BUNGALOW—ANECDOTE.

CHAPTER III.

Paget and I spent a very pleasant week in Bombay. We lunched at Government House, Malabar Point, that most delightful of residences. It consists of several bungalows grouped together amidst trees and shrubs on a high promontory with lovely views all round and the sea beating against the rocks below. There is always a breeze, no matter how hot the day; but during the monsoon it blows so strongly that it is almost impossible to live here, and the trees on the north side grow lob-sided in consequence. However, at the season of which I am now writing, what with the poincettias and bourgonvillias in full bloom, the garden of geraniums and other flowers, and the fine banian-trees which are here so carefully tended, and the beautiful little striped squirrels running about all over the place, it seemed an earthly paradise. These squirrels had for me a great charm all over India. They are everywhere, and so tame that they will run about one's room, and add perpetual animation to the scene.

At the end of the week we went to Poona. This, our first journey on an Indian railway, was most interesting to us. Leaving the Byculla station at two p.m., we met two of our Peninsular and Oriental fellow-passengers in the train. All the railways in India keep Madras time, which, being half-an-hour earlier than that at Bombay, makes it somewhat awkward for people not accustomed to think of the difference and who naturally rely on their watches; the consequence on this occasion was that we very nearly missed our train.

The railway-carriages are all arranged as sleeping compartments to hold six people, the upper berths coming down at night; but when they are full, which fortunately is seldom the case, are not very comfortable, for with the heat and dust of

India, and the amount of bedding and small packages usually carried, space is most essential. On this occasion, although only four, it was lucky that we were not to pass the night in the train, for our 'boys' crammed so much luggage of all sorts into the carriage that we looked very much as if we were travelling in a luggage-van.

In India everyone carries about his bedding, so that also takes up a considerable space. I remember on one occasion forgetting mine, or rather, I may say, thought it was unnecessary to take it, as I was going to stay at a large Residency. I arrived late, and on going to bed, found I was only supplied with a mattress and pillow, without a pillow-case. It being very cold, I covered myself with the room carpet, and slept soundly.

It was excessively hot during the first part of our journey from Bombay to Poona, but on reaching Kalyan we began to ascend the ghauts, and then the air became sensibly cooler and the scenery very fine. These hills are covered with teak and mango-trees, with a dense undergrowth of jungle, the haunts of many tigers, panthers, and sambur, but the jungle is always so thick that it is next to impossible to get at them, and so they mostly live a life of peace to themselves, whilst preying on the cattle to a great extent. The railway passes over bridges with the valley lying one thousand to fifteen hundred feet beneath, and in places gives one a very unpleasant feeling of insecurity. There were one or two horrible accidents when it was first opened, but now every possible precaution is taken, so that really there is no danger. My barometer showed a rise of two thousand feet between Bombay and Karjat, and Poona itself is about nineteen hundred feet above the sea.

We arrived at Poona at half-past seven. Here again we had been made honorary members of that most excellent establishment, 'The Club of Western India.' Comfortable bed-rooms, a lovely house and garden, an excellent dinner at a most moderate price, and, last but not least, the company of some pleasant members, and what more could we desire?

Coming from the heat of Bombay we felt the cold a good deal, but, after all, it was seventy-two degrees in our rooms at night.

The next day we spent in driving about the native bazaar, looking at the kinkob manufactory and buying several pieces of this most beautiful stuff. It is a mixture of gold thread and silk interwoven, and is made here to perfection in the most artistic patterns. It is very expensive, ranging from thirty-four to fifty rupees a yard, but, when one considers the labour and the amount of gold used, it is not really extravagant, especially to people drawing money from England; for, the rupee having now gone down to sixteen-pence, anyone banking at home at this price gains forty per cent.

No wonder poor, hard-working Indians grumble, when sending home money for the education of their children, at being mulcted forty per cent. for it.

We drove out to Parvati's temple on a hill four miles off; but beyond the view, which is fine, and the fact that it is from this spot that the last Guicowar, in 1817, saw his army defeated by the British in the Battle of Kirkee, there is nothing very remarkable about it.

We were anxious to see Hyderabad in the Deccan, and, having received a telegram from Mr. Cordery, the Resident there, inviting us to spend a few days with him, we left Poona by the half-past seven train on the evening of December 7th. This time we had a carriage to ourselves, and passed a comfortable night, arriving at Wadi junction, where the main line branches off for Madras, at half-past eight the next morning. At most Indian stations they have very good refreshment rooms, and we found that Wadi station was no exception in this particular, for they provided us with an excellent repast, and sent us off happy as we got into the train of the Nizam's state railway at ten o'clock.

I was much struck with the beauty of the

stations on this line. Each of them is a perfect garden; a blaze of flowers and beautiful shrubs. Roses, crotons, poincettias in masses, and the beautiful foliage of the banana and various palms towering above them, whilst the trellis-work of the station bungalows was covered with a blue convolvulus, of a size and of an intense hue never to be seen in our cold climate. A great majority of the plants and shrubs are in pots, in fact the gardens in India are essentially pot-gardens, for in this way they can be moved and protected from the intense sun in the hot season, and the heavy rain during the monsoon.

The company on this line have a good system of giving money prizes to the station-masters for the best-kept gardens, which, while a source of profit to themselves—in that besides the prize they can make money by selling plants—renders travelling far more agreeable than it would be if the eye had nothing to rest on but the glare and dust of the natural Indian landscape. It is interesting to watch the different birds along the line. Most of them do not seem to take the slightest notice of the passing train, but sit perched upon the telegraph wires, quite indifferent to the noise and smoke of the engine and carriages. Of the numerous kinds the most common are the king-crow, with its long black tail, the feathers bending out like those of a blackcock; the green and yellow merops, or bee-eater; and the beautiful blue jay, which, as it opens its wings and flies away, displays its lovely colour to perfection. The impertinent mynahs are of course to be seen strutting about in every station and village, looking as if they thought the whole place belonged to them.

The country is flat and uninteresting until within four miles of Hyderabad, where the jungle begins. The mixture of foliage of peepul and mango-trees, and the toddy and cocoa-nut palms, makes the scene wild and attractive. About fifteen miles from Hyderabad, a curious formation is reached. The whole plain is covered with large rocks, at the top of which huge rocking stones, weighing several tons, are to be seen. They look as if an ordinarily high wind would blow them over, so fragile is the base upon which they stand; and yet they have endured century after century. This formation of country is the same all the way to Hyderabad, and gives one the idea of a series of ruined cities.

We arrived about five p.m. Mr. Cordery had sent his carriage to the station for us, and we drove at once to the Residency, which is about a mile-and-a-half off. It is an imposing-looking building, standing in a large compound in a suburb called Chudderghaut. The house reminds one somewhat of the British Museum, and a curious fact about it is that a great deal of the furniture, and in particular all the gilt chairs in the front hall, came from the Pavilion at Brighton, where it was sold. We were most hospitably received, and nothing can exceed the comfort and luxury of the house.

The evening of our arrival there was a large dinner-party, given by one of the great Hyderabad nobles—the Nawab Vikar Ul Umra—to which we were invited. So at half-past seven we started in a carriage and four horses with Mr. Cordery, Lord Fife, Mr. Ogle (who were staying at the Residency), Colonel and Mrs. Rawlins, and several others, escorted by a guard of honour of sowars of the Hyderabad contingent.

A very few years back it was most dangerous for a European to enter the native city, and even now no one but natives can do so without an order from the Resident. But things have become much quieter, and, beyond the occasional meeting with a fanatic running amuck, there is little or no danger in visiting the town. As we drove along, I could not help remarking how thoroughly Oriental the whole place had remained, much more so than most of the big Indian cities. We passed some fine buildings, and the town looked tidy and clean. Our coachman drove uncommonly well, steering us through the narrow, crowded, and winding streets in a wonderful manner to our host's house, which is about two miles from the Residency.

The Nawab, with his English private secretary, Dr. Lauder, received us at the door. He is a good-looking man of about thirty, with a charming manner, and speaking English fluently. He led the way to a beautiful suite of rooms, furnished in English style, and introduced me to his son, a nice, intelligent boy of ten years old, who also speaks English well, and who, next year, is to be sent to school in England, to complete his education at Eton.

The dinner and wines were excellent, and a good band discoursed some lovely music during the meal. We sat down a party of about thirty people, and after dinner adjourned to a large marble court, with a tank full of gold fish, and fountain in the middle, and illuminated with hundreds of small oil-lamps of various colours. Here, whilst we were drinking our coffee and smoking our cheroots, a nautch-dance was performed before us by the *élite* of the Hyderabad dancing-girls, who were covered with heavy bangles and jewellery from head to foot.

The Nawab talked to me for some time. He, as I before mentioned, has a charming manner, and expresses himself very well in English, and is, I hear, a fine rider and polo-player; in fact, takes great interest in all sports. Hearing that Paget and I were both looking forward to getting some big-game shooting, he kindly asked us if we would join the party he was getting up at the end of February or beginning of March, when he proposed passing six or seven weeks in the jungle. He told us that everything would be provided, and that all we had to do was to bring our rifles and bedding. Such a proposal is not come across every day, and we eagerly accepted his kind offer. Dr. Lauder was also very nice about it, and, as he is to make all the 'bandobast,'* or arrangements, he told us to write to him about anything we wished to know concerning the expedition.

We were also introduced to another agreeable native gentleman, Nawab Said Hussein, well known as a thorough English scholar, and a

* Pronounced bunderbust.

man whose opinion is much valued in most matters. I have hardly ever met a more pleasant companion; and, hearing that we were fond of sport, he promised to organise a black-buck hunt with cheetahs for our amusement.

As we left the Nawab's house, he presented each of his guests with three or four bottles of attar of roses. This is a very old Hyderabad custom, which, though dying out in some houses, is always strictly kept up by the Vikar Ul Umra.

Next day was spent in driving through the city to the great Meer Alem tank, which is about eleven miles long, and supplies water to the whole country round. Like many of these large Indian lakes, or tanks, it is formed by damming up a valley with what is called a bund, and so keeping in the water during the rains. In this case the bund is well worth an inspection, as it is built of very strong stone arches, like a bridge lying on its side. The city was even more picturesque by day than by night, and the variety of costumes, the men armed to the teeth, the crowds of elephants and camels, made it altogether a gay sight. Numbers of fakirs, or religious beggars, implored us for alms in loud, sing-song voice, as we passed. The crowds were so dense in some of the streets that it was with difficulty we could get the horses and carriages through them. The handsomest building in the town is the Chuhar Minar, a lofty tower two hundred and fifty feet high at the junction of the four city main streets.

We drove out and visited the tombs of Golconda, which are about five miles off. They stand in well-kept compounds full of orange and guava-trees, and are very handsome; like all Mahomedan tombs, they are dome-shaped and covered with inscriptions from the Koran. Some of them were also decorated with a pattern in blue and yellow enamel, painted on earthenware. I regret to say that little of the original now remains, but what does is as fresh in colour as on the day it was made. I picked up some pieces that were lying on the ground, knocked down, probably, by the parrots which have made these tombs their regular abode, and kept flying about shrieking from every crevice.

The town of Golconda now only consists of a fort and palace of the Nizam, built on a rocky hill about two miles from the tombs. I had always imagined, in common with many others, that the famous diamond-mines of Golconda were situated here, but I was now undeceived, and discovered that there never were any diamond-mines at Golconda, although these precious stones were formerly brought here and stored in great quantities with the Nizam's treasure, and consequently the place got the reputation of producing the stones; the real Golconda mines were situated on the coast of Coromandel, a little to the north of Mazulipatam.

A curious sight in the Residency gardens is the colony of flying foxes. They hang all day from the branches of two large trees, and look like so many black bags. At night they fly about and feed upon any fruit which they can pick up. We threw stones and disturbed them for a short time, but after flying about for a few minutes in a very lazy and heavy way, pursued by the crows, they invariably returned to their former perches in the trees.

The morning of December 11th, Paget and I were up early, and at seven o'clock drove off to Major and Mrs. Nevill's house, to see his regiment of African cavalry.

They are all recruited from the Somali coast, and are veritable black negroes, fine, tall, strong-looking men, but, I should imagine, much more useful as infantry than as cavalry, for they certainly did not seem at home on their horses, which I thought were very badly bitted, the bits in most cases being far too large and heavy for such small animals.

They did some wheels very creditably, but in the charge two men cut voluntaries and four or five lungís were left on the battle-field.

The band of the regiment, also composed of blacks under a German band-master, played exceedingly well. After the drill, Mrs. Nevill, who is a daughter of the late Charles Lever, the famous novelist, gave us some 'chota hazri,' and took us to see her tame sambur, and at ten o'clock we drove back to the Residency.

At eleven o'clock we left again, with Mr. Cordery and a guard of honour, to lunch with His Highness the Nizam. He is the greatest of the Indian sovereigns, the Guicowar of Baroda coming next, and the Maharajah Holkar being the third. The city palace is neither grand nor imposing in any way, in fact the approach looks very much like that to an ordinary private-house. We were received by an aide-de-camp in green uniform and aiquillettes, who led us up some steps into a verandah, where the Nizam was seated. He came forward and shook hands with us. He is a small-built and delicate-looking young man, with black beard and long hair hanging down his back. He seemed shy of talking English, but all he said was well expressed.

Since my visit, the Nizam's name has come very

prominently before the British public by his display of unexceptional talents in the way of government, and also by his thorough, business-like ways. He goes heart and soul into all matters affecting his people, and is exceedingly popular and highly respected all over the country. He has a great opinion of Englishmen, and is lucky in having such advisers as Mr. Cordery and Colonel Marshall.

His late magnificent gift of sixty lacs of rupees, or four hundred thousand pounds, towards the defences of India, proves above all things how loyal he is towards England. Besides possessing statesman-like qualities, he is a very fine rider, a first-rate shot, and good at tent-pegging and polo.

We were a party of twenty at lunch, and I sat at the Nizam's right and Mr. Cordery on his left. The meal consisted of a large variety of Oriental dishes, most of them very rich and full of spice; but the pilau and curries were excellent. Amongst the latter was an orange currie, quite a new dish, which I was told was made in honour of us, but I cannot say that I cared much for it. I talked to the Nizam a great deal about sport. He told me that he had heard we wished to see a cheetah-hunt, and had arranged one for us for the next day.

After lunch, we smoked our cheroots on the verandah, and His Highness had the whole of his stud trotted out for our inspection. We looked at about one hundred Arabs, Walers, and native-bred horses, some of the former being the handsomest I have ever seen, and all wonderfully broken by the native stud-groom.

That evening we dined with our friend Nawab Said Hussien, in his comfortable new house in Chudderghaut. He had a wood-fire burning in one of the drawing-rooms, thinking it would remind us of home, and after dinner we witnessed a series of nautch-dances, both Mahomedan and Hindoo. These entertainments are somewhat disappointing, the women are generally very ugly, the music, singing, and dancing are most monotonous. The nautch troupe consists of two or more women who dance and sing to an accompaniment played by the men on the tomtom, flute, and a kind of fiddle. The dancers have their ankles covered with heavy bangles, so that it must be very tiring work. In intervals of the dance they chant a monotonous song, clapping their hands the whole time, and generally have a large piece of betel-nut in their mouths. On this particular evening the performance began with a Mussulman troupe, followed by another one of Hindoos, but the dances were all much alike, and we soon had enough of them.

We were introduced to another native gentleman, Mahomet Ali Beg, now Assur Jung, secretary of the Nizam, and famous through India as one of the best riders and sportsmen of the whole empire. He was to conduct the cheetah-hunt in the morning.

Next day we left the Residency at seven o'clock in three carriages for our hunting expedition. Besides Paget and myself, our party was made

HUNTING BLACK BUCK WITH CHEETAHS

up of Mr. Cordery, Mr. and Mrs. Cornish, Mrs. Stead, Mr. Herbert Gladstone, Mr. Tennant, Mr. Maxse, Mr. Winthrop, Herr Von Dyke, and Dr. Du Bois, with Mahomet Ali Beg to show us the sport. After a drive of five-and-twenty minutes, we came to a large maidán, or plain, covered with long grass and shrub, and here we left our carriages, some of us mounted elephants, while others got on the horses which had been sent on. I had never been on an elephant, and was anxious to make the experiment, so I chose it instead of a horse. The beast was made to kneel down, a ladder placed at his side, and Mrs. Stead, Mr. Cordery, and I got into the howdah. The sensation as the elephant gets up is very odd, it feels as if you were being thrown backward and then forward again, like a shuttle-cock. The motion in walking is not unpleasant, though now, after a good deal of experience, I am bound to say there is a vast difference between a rough and a smooth animal.

The cheetahs were tied on common native

bullock-carts, and hooded. We did not move until we had given them a good start, then, following slowly about four hundred yards behind, we traversed the plain spying for game. It seems that the black buck are so used to seeing bullock-carts in the ordinary course of work that they take little or no notice of them.

And such was the case in this instance. On spying a herd, we on the elephants and horses immediately halted about four or five hundred yards off, whilst the carts went slowly on, getting gradually nearer and nearer to the game. When within seventy yards the cheetah was unhooded, and on seeing the quarry bounded off at a tremendous pace and pulled a buck down by the throat. The shikari then ran up, cut the animal's throat, and fed the cheetah with the blood collected in a tin basin. We had two stalks, and then, being engaged to breakfast with the Nawab Vikar Ul Umra, we left off, and went back home as we came. I was rather disappointed in the sport, for I had expected to see more of a run between the cheetah and buck, whereas it was all over in a few seconds after the cheetah was unhooded.

Changing at the Residency, we drove to the Vikar's garden between four or five miles off. Here, in a lovely kiosk, surrounded with shrubs and flowers of all sizes and colours, was served a real Persian breakfast. The courses seemed endless; some dishes were really excellent, whilst others I should require a good deal of education in Persian cookery to like. Saffron was the prevailing flavour, and all were rather greasy and rich. Breakfast over, we drove up the hill to see the Vikar's new palace; it is not nearly finished, and has already cost six lacs of rupees. The hill is all of solid rock, and the Vikar is making a garden round the palace, every particle of soil having to be carried up, and pipes for water also laid the whole way. The stables are good, and full of fine-looking animals. On leaving, we were again all presented with bottles of attar of roses, and returned to the Residency after spending a pleasant day.

I do not know when I spent a more agreeable time than I did at Hyderabad under Mr. Cordery's hospitable roof. Each day we went for drives in the neighbourhood, and passed many a delightful hour with the officers of the different regiments quartered at Secunderabad and Tremulgherry, so that it was with sincere regret that I said good-bye to my host and took the train back to Poona; but having received a telegram from the Duke of Connaught's aide-de-camp, saying that Their Royal Highnesses would be there on the following morning and wished me to meet them at the station, I had no time to spare. Paget travelled with me as far as Poona, going straight on to Bombay. He wished to see Burmah, and so we parted, agreeing to meet again at Hyderabad at the end of February, for our big-game shooting expedition with the Nawab Vikar Ul Umra.

The following months I spent chiefly with the Duke and Duchess. I accompanied them in the Duke's tour of inspection all through the Bombay Presidency, and saw the places of interest under most favourable circumstances. Their Royal Highnesses received a most loyal and hearty welcome everywhere, but nowhere more so than in Kathiawar, where the young nobles of the Rajkot college, at their own special request, formed a guard of honour and escorted their illustrious visitors into their city.

We returned to Bombay from this tour on the 3rd of February, and were encamped at the Cooperage, the head-quarters of the commander-in-chief when in Bombay. His Royal Highness Prince Frederick Leopold of Prussia, the Duchess of Connaught's brother, Count Kanitz, and Major von Nickisch were also of our party there, and we altogether formed a very large camp. Bombay was most agreeable just then, with a lot of gaieties coming on; but I was anxious to see the north of India, so most reluctantly I left, and went through Rajpootana, part of the north-west provinces, and the Bengal Presidency.

Never did I know before what real hospitality meant. In England, when we have asked a stranger to dinner or lunch, we think we have been very civil, and done all that can be expected of us; but in India one finds houses open, and people ready to give you their best, pressing you, in good faith, to stay as long as possible. Wherever I went I was received in this kind and hospitable manner, and I thoroughly enjoyed my trip from beginning to end.

In this short sketch of my visit to India I have purposely avoided giving descriptions of places, native customs, and ceremonies, all so well known to readers of books of Indian travel, and of which many who have not even witnessed the scenes may know more than I, who have visited them. I shall therefore confine myself mostly to incidents which happened to myself.

On my visit to Delhi, I had a letter of introduction to one of the chief officials, but I had a friend with me who had resided there for some time, and he proposed that we should go to the dâk bungalow and be thoroughly independent.

We arrived at Delhi after dark, and, walking straight from the station to this bungalow, were disappointed to find it quite full. We therefore had to go to a dirty and uncomfortable little place, rejoicing in the grand name of the Great Northern Hotel. The food was quite uneatable, and we took all our meals at the refreshment-room of the railway-station.

The morning after our arrival, and whilst I was cursing my fate at being in such an uncomfortable place, my boy announced the manager of the dâk bungalow, who came to inform me that he now had a vacant room, which I agreed to go and see as soon as I was dressed. Off we went accordingly; but, on getting there, the first thing that met our eyes was a police-officer packing up and sealing luggage in the room that was to be mine.

I asked him what was the matter, and he quietly answered,

'A gentleman died here last night. We are moving his things. The body was taken away just now, and the room will be quite ready for you gentlemen in ten minutes.'

He could give us no information as to what the poor old man had died of, and although, afterwards, we found out that it was from heart disease, and that his death had occurred in his carriage whilst driving from the Kootab and not in this room; yet, as we did not learn these details at the time, we preferred to stay in the hotel, bad as it was.

CHAPTER IV.

AGRA—JUBILEE DAY—GRAND PARADE OF TROOPS—THE GAOL—CARPET MAKING—GYMKANA MEETING—BHURTPORE—JUBILEE PROCESSION—MAHARAJAH'S DURBAR AND DINNER—FIREWORKS—LOYALTY OF NATIVE PRINCES—BENARES—INDIAN HOTELS—MADDESSAR KOTHI—RAJAH SIVAPRASAD—HIS AVERSION TO BENGAL BABOOS—SIGHTS OF BENARES—THE SACRED MONKEYS—MR. DAVIS DEFENDS MADDESSAR KOTHI AGAINST VIZIER ALI—MR. DAVIS'S GALLANT DEFENCE OF MADDESSAR KOTHI—RIVER SIGHTS—LEAVE FOR POONA AND HYDERABAD.

CHAPTER IV.

On Jubilee Day, the 16th of February, I was staying at Agra with Dr. Tyler, governor of the gaol there. The day was kept as a general holiday throughout all India, the natives seeming to enter thoroughly into the spirit of the auspicious occasion, and certainly Agra was no exception to the rule. Early in the morning four hundred prisoners were to receive their liberty; so I went over the gaol to see them, Dr. Tyler sitting at a desk and ticking off their names as they came up, whilst their female relatives were squatting down outside the big gates waiting for them. I took the opportunity of going round the whole of the prison, which is an immense building, and very well kept. I saw large gangs of prisoners squatting in the various yards, and amongst them a number of Burmese dacoits, who were easily to be distinguished from the rest by their high cheek-bones and thorough Malay type. They were about as unprepossessing a looking lot as I ever gazed on.

Agra gaol is famous for the carpets made by the prisoners, and I went over most of the looms. There were some very fine ones in progress for Princess Beatrice, Prince Frederick Leopold, Count Kanitz, and others, though they did not advance very quickly, for just then many of the prisoners who did this particular work had been liberated; but Dr. Tyler told me most of them would be back in prison before the year was out, and this, I afterwards heard, was the case all over India, for the majority of the criminal classes live a much more comfortable life in prison than out of it.

There was a grand parade of troops in Agra that morning, but, as I had not brought my uniform with me, I could not attend it. I lunched with General Rogers, the commandant, at its conclusion, after which I went on to the Gymkana meeting, where a huge crowd was assembled to see the various sports, consisting of Ecca and buffalo races, and other eccentric and amusing games. But we had been invited by the Maharajah of Bhurtpore to spend Jubilee evening with him at his capital, so we drove off to the station. The Duke and Duchess of Manchester and Lady Alice Montagu were of our party, which was large enough to fill several carriages of a special train.

Reaching Bhurtpore station at six o'clock, we were met by the Resident, Colonel Euan Smith, a quantity of carriages, and an escort of the Maharajah's sowars. We drove to the Residency, dressed for dinner, and, again entering our carriages, drove in procession through the bazaar.

The whole town was illuminated with thousands of little oil-lamps, stuck into trellis-work made of bamboo, all along the side-walks, and had a very pretty effect. On arriving at the police-station we got out of our carriages and went to a long balcony, also illuminated with these lamps, and as we sat there the procession filed past down the street. It was headed by eight elephants most gaudily decorated; these were followed by a native band of music, and then came a regiment of sowars, again eight more elephants, amongst which was one with a golden howdah and covered with kinkob, or cloth of gold from head to foot. The Maharajah sat in this howdah, and, as he passed our balcony, stood up and bowed.

The procession being over, we again got into our carriages, drawn by four horses, and proceeded to the palace. We were all presented to the Maharajah, who held a grand Durbar, in which Colonel Euan Smith read a letter from the Viceroy thanking His Highness for all his loyal expressions on this auspicious occasion, and at nine we sat down to a magnificent banquet in the large hall. The Maharajah, being a strict Hindoo, was not present at the dinner, but as soon as the dessert was handed round he came in and sat next Colonel Euan Smith, who rose, and, in a very eloquent speech, proposed the Queen-Empress's health. The toast was most loyally drank, and then the Duke of Manchester gave the Maharajah's health, which was also received heartily. After dinner we adjourned to the terrace and witnessed a really fine display of fireworks; these were followed by a nautch-dance in the Durbar-room, and at one o'clock in the morning we again left for Agra in a special train, having passed an interesting day.

The jubilee had been celebrated in similar ways all through this vast empire, the native chiefs vieing with each other, and showing their loyalty by the magnificence of the tomasha. This display should have done a great deal to dissipate the foolish fears of the croakers who imagine that these maharajahs and chieftains are hostile to our rule in India. By the enormous sums they have spent in celebrating the Queen-Empress's jubilee, I think they have clearly shown that such is not the case.

Of all the cities I visited in India, Benares struck me as the most interesting. Situated on the sacred river Ganges, it is the chief of the sacred cities, and thousands of pilgrims flock from all parts of India to bathe from the ghats. It is esteemed a blessed thing amongst Hindoos to die at Benares, and plunging sick persons into the water is the cause of a good many deaths. The town is picturesque, and the streets near the river are excessively narrow, everyone wishing to be as near as possible to the sacred stream.

I arrived at Benares at a quarter to nine on the morning of the 20th of February, and drove straight to Clarke's Hotel, where I was received by the proprietress, a showily-dressed lady, with an ebony complexion, who seemed to think she was doing a great act of condescension in permitting me to enter her house.

It surprises me to note how bad Indian hotels are as a rule. It is true that owing to the kindness and hospitality of friends I did not visit many of them, but the few I stayed in, with the exception of the Royal Hotel at Lucknow, were horrible and filthy places. Watson's Hotel at Bombay is about as uncomfortable a hostelry as is to be found anywhere in the civilized world, yet everyone goes there because it is the best in the place. Everyone grumbles, and I only wonder no one has the enterprise to establish a really first-rate hotel at Bombay, for I am confident a fortune might be made out of it.

After dressing and breakfasting with a considerable party of globe-trotters, a card was brought me from Mr. Akshaya Kumur Mitra, the private secretary of the Maharajah of Benares, and I found him waiting in the hall. He told me that he had orders from the Maharajah to take me to one of his palaces, and to see that I wanted for nothing. I soon put my things together, and was not sorry to see the last of Clarke's Hotel.

The palace in which I was put up is called Maddessar Kothi. It has large lofty rooms, is comfortably furnished, and surrounded by a lovely flower-garden. The eves of the house are the haunts of a numerous colony of green parrots, who kept up a continual concert, and occasionally even came into the rooms. I was all alone in this house, save the servants, twenty in number, and felt rather like a state prisoner. When at Poona, Lady Winford had kindly given me a letter of introduction to the Rajah Sivaprasâd of Benares, so I sent this off by a messenger, and at four o'clock received a visit from this most charming and interesting old gentleman. In the course of conversation he told me that the dream of his life was to visit England, but that being a very high caste Hindoo this was impossible, for by his religion he would lose caste were he more than three days at sea.

'Oh,' he said, 'if they would only make a railway I would go at once; or even if I were now ordered to give evidence in London on a Royal Commission on Indian Affairs I could go, for a man obeying the government does not lose caste.'

He took me in his carriage to see all the sights of this wonderful city. We went to the college, a fine Gothic building about fifty years old, and then threaded our way through the brass-workers and kinkob-makers to the golden temple, followed by a dense crowd of fakirs and pilgrims shouting for 'backsheesh.' The most curious sight of all is the cow temple, where a lot of sacred bulls and cows are tied up round the inside of the place, which in consequence smells much more like a farm-yard than a place of worship. Some of these animals are so old that they can hardly see or stand. Wreaths of flowers are sold to the visitors, who feed the beasts on them. I visited the well of knowledge, a very smelly hole, and added some flowers to the many thrown in by the pilgrims; then again we threaded our way through the crowds to the Manmandira Observatory, where I had a splendid view of the river and ghats from the platform at the top. We now returned to our carriage, and drove to the monkey temple a little way off. In this large, red-brick building are innumerable sacred monkeys, which come down to be fed by boys with plates of fruit, but they get so much to eat that they are decidedly dainty. The monkeys had increased so rapidly that, a short time before my visit, many of them had been caught and transported to the other side of the river.

As I drove home that evening, Rajah Sivaprasâd informed me that there was a very interesting event connected with the house where I was staying, and gave me a small book with an account of it, which I read during my solitary dinner that night. As it may probably interest my readers, I will here give a short *résumé* of the way in which Mr. Davis, on the 14th of January, 1799, defended this house with a single spear against the rebel ex-king of Oude, Vizier Ali, and a following of three hundred men.

In 1798, the British found it necessary to depose Vizier Ali, King of Oude, on account of his numerous excesses and his misgovernment. They, however, granted him a large pension, *viz.*, a lac and a half of rupees, about fifteen thousand pounds, and settled him in Benares as a resident. Here, on the borders of his former kingdom, surrounded by a numerous retinue, he began intriguing against the British, with the object of getting back into power. At length the government awoke to the danger of leaving him so near to Oude, and ordered him to Calcutta, entrusting the execution of the order to Mr. Cherry, the political agent of the Governor-General. Unfortunately for himself, Mr. Cherry could not be brought to see that Vizier Ali meant any mischief; but on the 13th of January, 1799, the native superintendent of police came and warned Mr. Davis, the judge and magistrate of the district, who lived in the house I was now occupying, that Vizier Ali was collecting a number of armed men, and had no intention of proceeding to Calcutta, as ordered by the government. Mr. Cherry was also given this information, and ordered the police to keep a watch on his movements.

Vizier Ali, suspecting that he was under surveillance, gave out that he would proceed to Calcutta in a day or two, and sent to tell Mr. Cherry that he would call on him next morning at breakfast.

Early the following day accordingly, Vizier Ali appeared, with a retinue of about two hundred men, but, as he was accustomed to go about with a large following, it did not alarm Mr. Cherry, who met him at the door, and showed Vizier Ali, who was accompanied by his friends Waris Ali and Izzut Ali, into his house. Mr. Evans, a private secretary to the government, was also there. Four armed followers entered the breakfast-room with the Vizier.

Mr. Cherry offered his guest some tea, but instead of drinking it, he began to complain of the treatment he had received from the late Governor-General, Sir John Shore, and said that he had been originally promised a pension of six lacs of rupees, which was now reduced to a lac and a half. He proceeded to upbraid Mr. Cherry for not looking after his interests; and, whilst this was going on, Waris Ali approached Mr. Cherry's seat. This seems to have been a signal arranged between them; for Vizier Ali now got up, and seized Mr. Cherry by the collar whilst his two friends held him down. As he tried to free himself, the other men rushed on him and cut him down with their swords. Mr. Evans was now attacked, but was rescued for the time by one of the Resident's attendants, and managed to leave the house, only, however, to be shot by the men outside. Captain Conway, another British officer, happening to come up at the time, was also killed.

Mr. Davis had been out riding that morning, and had passed Vizier Ali and his followers on their way to Mr. Cherry's; he, however, like that unfortunate gentleman, was in nowise alarmed at the numerous retinue. On getting home, the head of the police came to inform him that Vizier Ali had been collecting armed men from the neighbourhood, so he at once despatched a note to Mr. Cherry to inform him of this circumstance.

Whilst waiting for an answer, he saw Vizier Ali and his party returning and some of them entering his compound, where they fired at the sentry, whom they killed. Without a moment's hesitation he sent Mrs. Davis and the two children with the servants to the terrace at the top of the house, whilst he searched for arms. He came across a spear which was lying in his bed-room, one of the kind used by the running footmen of India. It was six feet long, with a triangular blade and sharp edges. With this weapon in his hands he rushed up the narrow, spiral staircase leading to the flat roof, where he had already sent Mrs. Davis with the two ayahs and children, and which could be closed at the top by a trap-door. In order not to expose the women to the fire from below he made them sit down close to this entrance, whilst he, pike in hand, looked down the steps, ready to give the first comer a warm reception. It was a long, narrow staircase, so that only one man could possibly mount at a time, and this gave Mr. Davis a considerable advantage.

Shortly afterwards steps were heard and one of the natives, with drawn sword, appeared at the bottom of the staircase and began to abuse Mr. Davis, whose only answer was that he had sent off for troops from camp and that they would soon be here. The rooms below were now full of armed men, and Mr. Davis, having shown himself, was instantly fired at, but without effect. The assault began in earnest, a man rushing up the stairs, but he got a hard prog from the spear and soon disappeared, and must have been seriously hurt for the stairs and the table-cloth in the room below were afterwards found covered with blood. The firing now began again, so Mr. Davis thought it prudent to draw on the trap-door, and, looking over the side of the terrace, he could see them on the verandah below trying to get a shot at him; but, finding this was impossible, they began to break the furniture. This noise was followed by a dead silence, and, thinking the enemy had withdrawn, one of the women looked over the parapet wall, but was at once shot through the arm.

Mr. Davis felt sure that the firing would have been heard in General Erskine's camp outside Benares, and was now anxiously waiting for the troops to come to his relief; but it was a dreadful time of suspense, for, although he had been already an hour on the roof, no signs of succour appeared. Soon again he heard footsteps of people coming up the stairs, and, drawing back the cover, was about to make a lunge with the spear when, just in time, he recognised one of his old servants coming up with plate which he had saved from the general wreck. This man was followed by the other servants and a native officer of his police with some sepoys. Finding he had now fifteen armed men, he considered the immediate danger over, although a police peon from the town brought news that Vizier Ali intended to renew the attack; he was now engaged in setting fire to European property in the neighbourhood. This respite was a lucky thing for Mr. Davis and his party, as, during the delay, a body of cavalry under Major Pigot and Captain Shubrick arrived, and they were soon followed by General Erskine and the remainder of the troops, who at once prepared to defend the house in case of attack.

Vizier Ali's party presently returned and fired several shots, under cover of a wood, but on the first shot from a field-gun withdrew to Madhoo Doss's garden, where they were pursued by General Erskine, who left a sufficient guard for Mr. Davis and the Europeans now collected together. The rebels were soon dispersed and the city recovered, but not without some loss to the British. The victims to Vizier Ali's treachery were five Englishmen, viz.: Mr. Cherry, Mr. Evans, Captain Conway, Mr. Robert Graham, and Mr. Hill, who had a shop in the city.

Vizier Ali succeeded in escaping for a time, and went off to Betaul, but he was eventually captured, and it is a singular coincidence that he was taken as a prisoner through Benares on the first anniversary of his revolt. He was interned first in Fort William at Calcutta, and afterwards in the fort of Vellore, and there died.

Next morning I inspected the staircase of the house, and found it exactly as described in the account of the massacre, the trap-door and the whole details of the place being in the same condition as in 1799.

The Rajah Sivaprasâd drove me down to the ghats, where we got on board a barge with paddles worked by men on the principle of an English tread-mill. In this we floated down the stream, and I witnessed one of the most picturesque sights. Hundreds of natives of both sexes and of all ages covered the wide flights of stone steps leading down to the river, whilst numbers of them were bathing in the sacred stream. Native music played from the terraces above, and worshippers threw garlands of flowers to float down the waters; pilgrims from all parts of India dressed in every conceivable colour added to the beauty of the scene.

The Rajah is a great admirer of the English government and a staunch Conservative, who has no patience with the ideas and aspirations of the young educated Indian, whom he would suppress as much as possible. On this subject we had long arguments. I maintained, and will always do so, that if we educate the native and thus enable him to reason freely, we must follow this up by giving him some share and interest in the government of his country, otherwise we are filling the land with a very dangerous element, viz.: a large population, increasing year by year, of men of the middle class, well-educated and without employment, men who care for their country, who have ideas of their own on the subject of reforms in government, and who yet have not the slightest opportunity of giving vent to these pent-up ideas.

The Rajah has a particular aversion to the Bengal Baboos, and sneered at them on every occasion. Talking of Lalmohun Ghose, who stood for Deptford at the last general election, he was much tickled when I said I supposed he would call him 'Lamentable Goose.'

We came across three human bodies floating about the river, with crows picking at them; it was a disgusting sight, and annoyed the Rajah very much, as it is now strictly forbidden to throw bodies in the river, but it is still done to a certain extent by the very poor in order to avoid the expense of cremation. The Rajah called the constables and pitched into them; then, turning to me, said,

'Here you have an example of the uselessness of a native in authority; if the police were English, such a thing could not occur, for they have strict orders to prevent it.'

We were now opposite the burning ghat. I had long wished to see the Hindoo funeral rites, and here they were in full force. Four bodies were being burnt, whilst four more came in, two men and two women. *Place aux dames* seemed to hold good, for they were disposed of first. The bodies were brought by the relatives on litters, and placed with their feet in the water of the Ganges. The relatives sprinkle water over the rest of the body, which is then taken out and placed on the logs of wood with more wood piled over them, and the whole set on fire. Meanwhile, the relations squat close by till all is burnt, when they throw the ashes into the river: the burning occupying from two to three hours. We landed, and looked at the sacred spring, a loathsome place, with the water as thick as pea-soup, where the pilgrims wash on first arrival. Again entering the boat, we floated further down, and saw a prostrate figure of a god, about thirty feet long, made of coloured sand. This figure is begun every November, and is washed away as the river rises during the following summer.

After staying at Government House, Allahabad, I returned to Poona, arriving there on the 24th of February. Here I met Captain Herbert, aide-de-camp to the Duke of Connaught, who was to be one of our party in our big-game shooting expedition.

We had hard work packing and making our arrangements, but, everything being ready, we left for Hyderabad by the half-past seven train on the evening of the 25th of February.

CHAPTER V.

ARRIVE AT HYDERABAD—DR. AND MRS. LAUDER AT CHUDDERGHAUT—MR. GERALD LODER—PREPARE FOR SHOOTING EXPEDITION—MY BATTERY—LIST OF ARTICLES MOST REQUIRED—POSTAL ARRANGEMENTS—A LARGE CORTÈGE—CURING SKINS—ASSUR JUNG—A COUNTRY LITTLE SHOT OVER—PANTHER SPEARING—ASSUR JUNG'S LITTLE SON.

CHAPTER V.

AFTER a hot and dusty journey, we arrived at Hyderabad at four o'clock in the afternoon of the 26th. At the station a chuprassi handed me a note from Dr. Lauder, in which he said that he had sent a carriage for us, and begged that we would come and stay at his house in Chudderghaut. He has a comfortable bungalow, surrounded by a garden, which, from being continually watered, was a mass of flowers and green grass. People who have not been much in the East can hardly appreciate how delicious this is to eyes that have been gazing for days on an arid and dusty landscape.

We were hospitably welcomed by Dr. and Mrs. Lauder, and introduced to Mr. Gerald Loder, who was staying in the house, and was to form one of our shooting-party in the jungle.

After a change, a drive through the city, and by the Meer Alem tank, we returned to the bungalow to dinner and a smoke in the verandah, at which the sole topic of conversation was our coming expedition. All of us, except Lauder, were quite new to big-game shooting; so that we drank in his anecdotes of former shikars with the greatest avidity, and he sent us all to bed dreaming of tigers, panthers, and other quarry.

Next day was devoted to overhauling our kits and seeing that everything was in order. My battery consisted of a ·500 Empress, by Holland and Holland, a No. 10 smooth-bore, by Moorson, and a pair of No. 12 smooth-bores, by Boss. I had ball-cartridges made for all my smooth-bores, and provided myself with an immense amount of ammunition from Rodda & Sons, of Calcutta. On an expedition like this, it is always as well to have a great deal more ammunition than is really required, for so many accidents may happen to it, carried about as it is on coolies' heads, or in rough bullock-bandies, through the jungle, and, as we should probably be between two and three hundred miles away from our base, it would have been very annoying to run short.

Dr. Lauder, who managed the whole expedition, made a most excellent bandobast, and seemed to have provided every luxury he could think of—such as champagne, hock, claret, sherry, two hundred dozen of soda-water, pâtés-de-fois-gras, liqueurs, and other similar things too numerous to mention. His Highness the Nizam kindly lent Paget and myself two of his staunch elephants, which, with the Vikar's three, had already gone on some days. The Vikar had also sent on eleven riding horses, three camels, seventy-two bullock-bandies, twenty sowars, and a like number of Rohillas, two complete sets of camp tents and cooks, and had arranged that we were to have a post backwards and forwards every two or three days, though sometimes this would entail a ride of from one hundred and fifty to two hundred miles for the sowars who carried it. We calculated that our party, including soldiers, servants, and followers, would number about two hundred and fifty men, a large body to move in a country with no roads, and where most of the provisions had to be carried about with us.

It was arranged that we should leave Hyderabad for our expedition on the 1st of March. We were therefore very busy the next two days after our arrival there, providing ourselves with the numerous but very necessary little things which one invariably puts off getting till the last moment. We ransacked Badham & Piles' large store at Secunderabad for solar-topes, cartridge-bags, &c., &c., and we bought several bottles of carbolic acid and some small glass syringes, for squirting any specimens of small birds we might like to keep, but did not care for the trouble of skinning. It is a dodge well worth knowing in a hot country, where nothing will keep more than three or four hours, and when one feels too lazy to go through the long and tedious operation of skinning. The method is as follows: As soon as the bird is killed, dilute some of the crystallized carbolic acid with water, put it in the syringe, and squirt down the bird's throat. The specimen should then be hung up for twenty-four hours in a place where no flies or ants can get at it; and then it may be put away. It will thus keep for months, eventually getting as hard as a stone.

I am here, however, bound to admit that these specimens give some trouble to the taxidermist afterwards; for they have to be thoroughly damped and softened before they can be skinned, and the feathers are apt to come out during the latter process; but when one considers how many beautiful birds are lost during the hot weather through the lack of energy to sit down and skin them after a long day's work, it is a great thing to have this simple plan of carbolic acid and a squirt to fall back upon. Great care should be taken in handling this acid, for it is very corrosive; and I had the unpleasant experience of losing the skin off two fingers, through letting some fall upon them. The least touch of it in the eyes will destroy the sight instantly.

People starting for the first time on a shooting expedition in India, are apt to take a quantity of useless things, and at the same time to omit some most necessary ones. I fell into this error; so, for the benefit of future shikaris who may follow in my footsteps, I will here give a few hints as to what I consider the things most required in the jungle. First of all, a good supply of flannel shirts, then a couple of shikari suits, made by a native darzi,* who will faithfully copy any pattern given to him, as demonstrated in the old Anglo-Indian story of the patched trousers. Two pairs of sambur leather boots, with cotton soles, are also useful for walking in the jungle: they prevent one slipping on the smooth rocks, and also deaden the crackling sound as one treads over the dry leaves. A

* Pronounced dersy.

couple of pairs of leather-gauntlets, with air-holes in the back, will save the hands from a good many scratches while riding through the thorny jungle; and a belt carrying a small pocket hatchet and saw, to clear the front on a tree, or to cut tempting-looking walking-sticks, will be found handy. Two solar-topes, and a pad to go down the back, are also absolutely necessary.

My shikari suits were made at a native shop in Bombay; the man supplied the stuff and made the whole suit for fourteen rupees, a little over one pound according to the value of the rupee at that time,—a not very extravagant price.

Last but decidedly not least of the comforts I had with me in the jungle was a spray diffuser and a good allowance of Penhaligon's bay rum. I cannot express how refreshing this was after a hard day in the hot jungle. So popular was it amongst our party that I got quite accustomed to see the different servants come to my tent as I was washing and changing for dinner in the evening, and saying, with their hands folded in front of them as though in prayer, 'Sahibs salaams please lend spray.'

I almost forgot to mention that it is as well to carry a thin gauze veil to keep the troublesome flies and bees off one's face and neck when sitting up in a tree waiting for big-game.

A large supply of arsenical soap and spirits of turpentine must be carried for preserving the skins; but, although it is absolutely necessary to use these two things freely on them when in the jungle, I must caution any future shikaris that it is quite as necessary to have the skins properly cured as soon as an opportunity occurs, and by no means to think of sending them home to England without doing so. I was told that my skins would keep as they were until they got home, and foolishly did not take the precautions I am here recommending; the consequence was that although on arrival I sent them at once to that excellent taxidermist, Mr. Ashmead, of Bishopsgate Street, they were very much damaged, and the following is an extract from the letter I got from him:

'We regret to say that the tiger skins have broken up in the dressing process, the leather having completely perished. We entrusted this work to the most experienced dressing firm. When no curatives have been applied, the heat of India appears to act on the fat on the skin, and the skin itself becomes technically burnt, and by keeping some months this tenderness becomes much worse.'

I do not pretend to have given a full and exhaustive list of all things required or even of those which are a comfort in the jungle, for it is difficult to remember afterwards things which at the time suggested themselves as being useful; but I merely mention some which are impressed upon my memory, and I hope my hints may prove useful.

All our preparations were completed on the 28th of February, and our heavy baggage and cartridges sent on that morning, we ourselves intending to start the next day; but in the afternoon the Nawab sent us word that he found the Nizam would require him on business, so that he could not possibly leave before the 2nd of March. This at first was a severe blow to us, as we were all keen to be off and have our first shot at a tiger; but there was nothing for us but to grin and bear it, and, I am bound to say, we had not much to complain of, as our lot had fallen in most comfortable and hospitable quarters.

Assur Jung Bahadur, better known to Englishmen as Mahomet Ali Beg, paid us a visit, and gave us a great deal of information about the jungle we were going to beat. He told us there were a good many wild elephants about, but he did not think our batteries were heavy enough for them. As it turned out, however, we did not come across any of these beasts, so it did not matter. He had much to say about panther spearing, a sport in vogue here, and somewhat dangerous to the novice, for the panther, unless speared in a vital part, is apt to turn round and charge horse and rider. Last November, when the Viceroy was at Hyderabad, they got up one of these meetings, and Lord William Beresford had what might have been a very nasty fall, the panther charging him and rolling him and his horse over, when it was luckily dispatched by Assur Jung.

Herbert got very much excited over the account of this sport, and was promised a day on his return to Hyderabad. He did get his day, but, on that occasion, there was also an accident, for the wounded panther sprang up a tree in which were a number of natives, and killed one of them.

We learnt from Assur Jung that it is a great many years since anyone shot over the district for which we were bound, and that there are an immense quantity of tigers about; in fact, from what I could learn, they seem to be very much on the increase all through India, for the native rulers are preserving them strictly in some parts, and will allow no one to shoot them without special permission. The Nizam himself has lately issued an order that the country fifteen miles round the Packall lake, a large piece of water about thirty miles long, is to be strictly preserved for him, and that no one is to shoot them on any pretence whatsoever; and so particular is he about it, that, although our host, the Nawab Vikar Ul Umra, is his brother-in-law, he would not give us leave to go over that particular district. As it is, there are a great many tiger, bison, and bear in the neighbourhood, and in the course of a few years, if they continue unmolested, that part will be simply overrun with them. They will kill all the cattle, so the people will perforce quit their villages and abandon their cultivated ground for securer habitations, and much now fertile land will soon revert to dense jungle.

We were all sorry to hear that afternoon that Assur Jung's plucky little son, a boy of eight, who is being brought up like an English boy and who is going to school in England with the Nawab Vikar Ul Umra's son, had had a fall off the horizontal bar whilst doing his gymnastic exercise, and had broken his arm. The brave little fellow never uttered a cry, and was carried off to the hospital, where his arm was set and he was going on well.

We had now given up all hope of Colonel Paget being able to join us here from Burmah before our start, but he, having telegraphed that he was on his way, Dr. Lauder had made all arrangements for him to catch us up in the jungle, by going to rail head and then riding on about fifty miles to our first shooting-camp, where we would wait for him.

CHAPTER VI.

OUR PREPARATIONS COMPLETED—WE LEAVE HYDERABAD—SCENERY ON ROAD—KAZAPET—LODER ILL—DINE AT STATION—LEAVE KAZAPET—RAILWAY NEARLY CONSTRUCTED—SINGARENNY COAL-FIELDS—DANGEROUS BRIDGES—ARRIVE AT RAIL HEAD—HOLY CITY OF POKUR—RIDE TO FIRST CAMP AT GALA—MANGO TOPES—TAPPAL AND NUZZER—JACKALS—PANTHERS—ANECDOTES OF SAME—MIDNIGHT VISITOR—LEAVE FOR NEXT CAMP—JUNGLE SCENERY—RIDE.

HYDERABAD STATION

CHAPTER VI.

At last our preparations were completed, and on Wednesday, March the 2nd, 1887, one of the fondest dreams of my life seemed about to be realised, for I was starting on a tiger-shooting expedition. I was as excited as when, a schoolboy, I was looking forward to shooting my first partridge, and six o'clock found me up and busy packing.

At half-past nine, Dr. Lauder, Herbert, Loder, and I drove to Hyderabad station, where we met our host, the Nawab Vikar Ul Umra, surrounded by a crowd of courtiers, retainers, and servants, some destined to accompany him, others come to wish him good-bye and God-speed. The platform was also covered with the numerous things which a native grandee and his suite always consider necessary for a journey. The retainers, and even the junior branches of a great man's family, in this country, are most servile and respectful in their manners, and not one of these people would think of addressing the Nawab without bringing his hands together as though in an attitude of prayer, and prefacing their sentence with the word 'Taxir,' which, being interpreted, signifies 'Guilty wretch that I am!'

This custom seems strange at first, but one soon gets so used to it as to feel almost inclined to copy it. The Nawab himself, when addressing the Nizam, who is his cousin and brother-in-law, invariably begins conversation with this formula, which it would be considered the height of presumption and ill-breeding to omit.

The train was already drawn up, and two first-class carriages of two compartments each reserved for our party, one for ourselves, into which our 'boys' were putting our bedding and bags, whilst the second was being prepared for the Vikar and his friends: a young Nawab, by name Murad

Hussein Khan, but we always called him 'Chota Nawab,' Mahomet Ismael Khan, master of the horse, Fuzlusul Khan, and Iman Ali Khan, two officers of the cavalry regiment. Besides these, there were numerous body-servants, pipe-bearers, valets, cooks, barbers, and such like.

The day was warm, and my thermometer soon rose to ninety-eight degrees in the carriage and well out of the sun. We passed through a wild and curiously formed country. Great rocks jutted out of the surrounding jungle everywhere. At a place called Bhonaghir, one of these rocks rises to a height of five hundred feet above the plain. It resembles a gigantic round shot, and is of the same colour. It has a face as smooth as glass, and on its summit stand the ruins of an old fort, access to which must have been most difficult.

The neighbouring jungle was very striking, for, though most of the trees were dried up and losing their leaves from the hot weather now just setting in, there were studded about amongst this brown mass two kinds covered with brilliant flowers, one a bright crimson and the other a lemon-yellow colour. It is a curious fact that, whereas with us the leaves fall in the cold, in India it is during the hot weather that Nature is dormant and the trees are leafless.

At one o'clock, during a long wait at the station, which is a disagreeable concomitant of Indian railway travelling, we opened our lunch-baskets and began tiffin. The Nawab sent a servant to us bearing four or five dishes of different kinds of curry. As a rule in India the curries are very mild, but in this case, though excellent, they were so hot one could scarcely eat them, and a few mouthfuls brought out beads of perspiration on our foreheads.

At half-past four we arrived at Kazapet. The line is open for traffic as far as Warungal, about six miles further on, but Kazapet is the head-quarters of the engineering staff, and the place from whence the trains of construction start every morning to rail head. As our carriages were to be attached to one of these trains the next morning, we remained here for the night. Mr. Molesworth, the resident engineer, gave us tea in his bungalow, and afterwards showed us his various hunting trophies, all the animals having been shot in this neighbourhood. He told us there were a great many bear in the rocks round the station, but, having sent on our guns and ammunition, we were obliged to leave poor Bruin in peace, and instead of going out shooting, we refreshed ourselves by taking a bath in the waiting-room of the station; for in India all the stations are arranged so that travellers can wash, sleep, and dress there. Dinner was spread on a table on the platform. It was excellent and did great credit to old Cassim, the Nawab's house steward and chief travelling cook, who throughout this expedition seemed literally to rise to the occasion, for the more difficulties he had to contend with the better was the result.

On this evening the insects were a perfect

pest, for as soon as the candles were lighted they came down in swarms; the table-cloth was made black with them, and we had to put plates over our tumblers to keep them out. Even then enough went down our throats to have caused the damnation of many a poor Jain, who, by his religion, being strictly forbidden to take life, wears a veil over his mouth to avoid the possibility of swallowing any animals floating in the air.

These insects were of all sizes and shapes, from the common, or garden-midge, to the large red cock-roach, and amongst them was a very peculiar one, looking like a needle on legs and which the natives call 'God's Horse.'

That night we slept in our railway-carriages, but it was so hot and close that I got very little sleep, besides which, Loder, who was in the same compartment as myself, was so ill and in such pain, caused by an internal chill, that at last I routed up Dr. Lauder, who gave him a strong dose of opium to relieve him.

At five o'clock next morning, we were attached to a construction train, consisting of a number of trucks full of iron sleepers, which are used all along this line instead of wooden ones, on account of the ravages made on the latter by the white ants; and now we made our start for rail head which was near Mankota, forty-five miles distant.

The line passes through dense jungle, which had only just been cleared sufficiently to allow of the rails being laid down. Huge trees, lately felled, lay everywhere at the sides, and large gangs of coolies were at work in many places. They looked with great astonishment at our carriages, never having seen anything of the sort before, and the women covered their faces with their veils, a habit they have when a sahib looks at them.

This line is a continuation of the Nizam's state railway, and will, eventually, be a connecting link between Hyderabad, Madras, and Nagpore, opening out a country very rich in minerals and agricultural produce, besides shortening the journey between Allahabad and Madras by many hundred miles.

At the time of which I am writing, the main object of the company was to get as quickly as possible to the newly discovered coal-fields of Singarenny. It is considered the best coal in India, the output was already very great, so that a large quantity had been collected at the pit's mouth, and was only waiting for the trains to carry it off. I forget the actual figures as to the output, given me by Mr. Molesworth, but at the time it struck me as being something enormous, and I should imagine that this company will be one of the best investments of the day.

The rails, as I have already mentioned, had only just been laid down, and but few of the permanent bridges had been built, most of those over which we passed being merely temporary structures, shored up with pieces of timber which looked anything but secure; and once or twice Mr. Molesworth felt rather nervous about them, and was not sure whether they would stand the weight and strain put upon them by our heavy carriages in addition to the trucks full of rails, so he insisted on remaining on the engine, where he could the better superintend our progress. Altogether it was rather exciting work, for we never could tell when we might find ourselves precipitated into a nullah, and a premature end put to our expedition. However, no *contretemps* occurred, and we arrived safely at rail head about half-past eight.

Here we found a large body of coolies and our horses all ready for us. After getting out the luggage and loading it on the backs of coolies, we started our 'boys' on foot, and, getting on the steeds, rode off for the first camp, at a place called Galah, some twenty-five miles off.

Loder's condition made us extremely anxious. He had been very ill all night, and was still in great pain. This long ride in the heat of the day was about the very worst thing he could do, under the circumstances; but there was no alternative, and we had great faith in the doctor, who remained with him, promising to bring him on slowly, after he had rested a short time in one of the engineers' tents, whilst we cantered on ahead, and saw that everything was comfortable for him in camp.

The Nawab had done everything in his power to make our expedition comfortable, and, amongst other things, he had sent men on some days previously, to place stones covered with chuman, or whitewash, on each side of the jungle path we were to follow, so that there was no fear of losing the way in the numerous tracts made by natives and wild animals, and which here serve the purpose of roads.

The Nawab, mounted on a beautiful Arab, and escorted by his personal friends, pipe-bearers, and four armed sowars, went on at once, but Herbert and I, being detained by poor Loder, started half an-hour later; we, however, caught him up after a few miles, and found him dismounted and smoking his hookah comfortably, under the shade of a huge tamarind-tree. We followed his example and also dismounted, not being at all sorry for half-an-hour's rest in the shade as the sun was terrifically hot, and, this being our first ride for some time past, we were not in as hard condition as desirable.

The jungle hereabouts was very grand with the number of big tamarinds and peepul-trees, large mimosas and clumps of bamboo, but never shall I forget the heat of that ride. The men entrusted with the work had marked out such a roundabout road that, after two hours, we struck the railway again only eight or nine miles from the place where we had left our train, whereas we must have ridden a good fourteen miles. This was annoying; however, there was nothing for it but to continue our ride on our now somewhat jaded steeds, and, after another short halt or two, we were much relieved to get the first glimpse of the camp pitched under a huge mango tope. This tope, or grove, consisted of from twelve to fifteen giant trees, which, from their size and the amount of shade given by their huge, spreading branches, must be very old. Close at hand were some paddie-fields and a running stream, whilst groves of toddy and cocoa-nut palms were dotted about the plain. Altogether, it was a lovely spot, and looked so fresh after our long, hot, and dusty ride.

Topes, or clumps of mango-trees, are very common all through India, for it is an article of faith that a good Hindoo should do three things, namely: beget a son, sink a well, and plant a mango-tope. How we blessed the memory of the pious man who had planted this one, but we had no voices for our benediction until after we had swallowed two or three iced whisky-pegs, as our throats were literally dried-up and parched with the heat and dust of the ride.

Mango-trees are useful in other ways besides that of giving shade, for they produce a large and valuable crop of fruit, and although these common mangoes are very different from those grown in Bombay, being stringy and with a strong taste of turpentine, yet the natives are fond of the fruit, and they are largely used for pickles and chutnee. The trees belong to the government and are farmed out to different people.

Our tents were comfortably arranged and furnished with beds and baths. A good tiffin was ready, to which we did ample justice, after which we passed most of the afternoon lying in our baths and on our beds.

Dr. Lauder and Loder came in about five o'clock; happily the latter seemed no worse for the journey, though very tired. We soon got him into a comfortable bed and to sleep.

The tapal, or head official of the village, came in to offer a nuzzar to the Nawab. This is the Indian homage from an inferior to a superior, and consists generally of a few coins laid on a piece of white linen or handkerchief, and presented in the palms of the hands. The great man to whom it is offered simply touches it and the donor then retires, but sometimes, to his dismay, the offering is taken. This the Nizam frequently does and gives it to a charity.

Our dinner-table was spread in a rice stubble-field, being more airy in the evening than under the trees. As soon as it was dark, we were greeted by most melancholy music from hundreds of jackals who had scented our whereabouts. These animals travel in large packs and exchange conversation with one another. One party is supposed to say, 'I smell the body of a dead Hindoo-oo-oo.' Then in the distance is heard, 'Where! Where! Where!' followed by the reply, 'Here! Here!' This noise goes on at intervals through the night, and the effect is weird and melancholy to a degree.

Our camp had been visited by a panther the previous night, so we tied up all the dogs for safety in our tents. Panthers seem to prefer dogs' flesh to any other, and, although naturally shy beasts, will come boldly into a camp at night after their favourite food. As an instance of the boldness of their pursuit of this quarry, even in the day-time, I may mention that when I was up at Mount Aboo in Rajpootana, in January, a lady and gentleman were walking close to their bungalow, accompanied by their favourite little dog, a fox-terrier, which was trotting on not ten yards in front of them, when suddenly they heard a rush, saw a cloud of dust in the road before them, and their pet was gone for ever. A panther had darted out of the jungle and seized him before their eyes and before they had even time to realise what had happened.

On the road between Ajmeer and the holy city of Pokur I saw numerous panther-traps let into the low walls by the side of the road, and made like gigantic mouse-traps, with a wretched dog tied up inside them as a bait. As soon as the panther seizes it the door of the trap comes down and leaves the two together as in a cage; very little of the poor dog remains when the trap is visited next morning.

Having mentioned the town of Pokur, I hope I may be excused a further digression in saying something about this interesting yet rarely visited place. It is in Rajpootana, about eight miles from Ajmeer, and is such a holy city that no life is permitted to be taken there. The consequence is that the birds are so tame they hardly take the trouble to move out of the way, and the streets are full of impertinent mynahs and thousands of blue pigeons. It contains a large sacred tank with ghats and temples on its borders, and there is also a fine temple to Brahma, the only one in this part of India. Hundreds of people of both sexes were bathing in the tank, which also supplies the drinking water.

On the occasion of my visit, I was staying with Major Creagh, V.C., commanding the Merwera battalion, who did such gallant service in the late Afghan war. He is well known and liked by the natives in this district, and had taken me through Pokur on our way to some famous duck and snipe ground where I enjoyed a good day's sport. On riding back, we were met at the outskirts of the town by four or five young women, carrying their lotas on their heads, dancing and singing. As I approached they came to my side and presented the lotas, in which I put a rupee. This is an ancient custom of greeting to a distinguished stranger, and is called a cullus. The stranger is supposed to give the rupee to the one he most admires, who thereupon considers herself his humble servant. I am bound to confess that I placed my rupee in the first lota presented, without reference to the ladies' charms. This may seem somewhat ungallant, but at the time I did not know as much about it as I do now. On re-entering the town, Major Creagh purchased some grain to feed the sacred pigeons, a proceeding which much pleased the inhabitants.

We turned in very early on our first night in camp, Herbert and I sharing the same tent. The heat was so great all the canáts were up; but, being tired, in spite of mosquitoes we were soon fast asleep. About one o'clock, I woke suddenly, with the sensation that something was moving close to me. I listened, and heard heavy breathing; it was certainly not Herbert. I tried to peer through the gloom, but could see nothing. At length I shouted to Herbert to get up, and, on our both looking round, we found two buffaloes coolly eating the straw on the floor of the tent and drinking the water out of our baths. Somewhat relieved that they were not wild or dangerous beasts—for we had no guns with us—we proceeded to drive them out, and presently were much amused at hearing them repeat their visit in the next tent, where Lauder and Loder were quietly slumbering.

At half-past five next morning, we were all up and dressed, and, after 'chota hazri,' Herbert and I mounted our horses, and started ahead of the rest of the party. In these parts it is most difficult to ascertain the distance from place to place. Everyone asked gives a different answer; and, whilst some said it was twenty, others put it at thirty miles between our first and second camps, the distance being calculated in coasts (a coast is about two miles). I afterwards calculated this morning's ride as twenty-five miles. And how delicious it was! I know of nothing so enjoyable as a ride in early morning through an Indian jungle. The air is fresh, and the whole country teems with animal life, whilst the scenery is so different from anything to be met with in Europe. This particular morning the sunrise, as seen through the jungle, was magnificent.

The trees about here were of a great size, and mostly covered with flowering creepers, amongst which I noticed passion-flowers of various kinds, and alamandas; every now and then we came upon the beautiful red and yellow flowering trees I had remarked on the road from Hyderabad to Warungal, and the air was scented with a sweet flower like jasmine. In the animal kingdom we passed numerous flocks of big Langoor monkeys, with their silky coats glittering in the sun, taking huge and seemingly impossible jumps from tree to tree, and yet never missing their mark. Peacocks and jungle-fowl darted into the dense jungle at our approach, whilst golden oriels, doves, and other bright birds flew about us. The seven-sisters, a kind of a shrike, which always move about in small families, from whence the name is derived, were of course there, as they are throughout India, but the oddest sight of all was a family of large hornbills sitting in solemn conclave on the branches of a big tree, and looking like so many wise judges. Never can I forget the pleasing impressions made on me by this my first morning's ride through the jungle, and this feeling was ever the same; so that through our expedition I looked forward to these early morning rides as one of its most agreeable features.

CHAPTER VII.

CAMP AT SIMALPAH—MEWAH-TREES—BEARS FOND OF THE FLOWERS—GREEN PIGEONS—ROSEATE-HEADED PARAQUETTES—KISHTIA, THE SHIKARI—NO KILL—MANNER OF SHOOTING TIGER IN THE DECCAN—PEAFOWL AND JUNGLE-FOWL SHOOTING—SHOOT GREEN PIGEONS—HALLAL CEREMONY—SEE TIGER'S TRACK—ROHILLAS AND TAME TIGER—PANTHER AND MONKEY—STORY OF PANTHER—DOCTOR IN CAMP—NO KILL AGAIN—BEAT FOR TIGER—POISONOUS SNAKES—ANECDOTES—RECOVERY FROM COBRA BITE—TELAGU SPOKEN.

CHAPTER VII.

About half-way through our ride we approached Singarenny, but, being anxious to get to the new camp, we merely skirted the village, and therefore saw nothing of the famous coal-fields. My poor pony soon afterwards began to show signs of distress; so I got off him, and rested a bit under the shade of a tree, when the Nawab and his party trotted up. Seeing how matters were, the Nawab mounted me on a beautiful waler which Ismael Khan had been riding, and, as he wished to remain there a few moments, asked him to put the animal through some of his tricks, to show me how thoroughly he had broken him in. It seems that this horse was bought at Calcutta, and had the reputation of being most vicious and unmanageable, but Ismael Khan, who looks after the Nawab's stud, has quite tamed him, and he is now quiet with everyone. He was made to lie down, get up again, and then, two of us taking a lungi, or turban, which we stretched out, each holding an end, Ismael jumped the horse over it. He had excellent paces, and was much more up to my weight than the small animal I had been riding, so that we got comfortably into our new camp in time for breakfast.

This, our first regular shooting-camp, was close to a village called Simalpah, situated in a valley at the foot of a range of hills covered with very thick jungle, the home of a large family of tigers which had been committing great ravages amongst the herds of cattle in the neighbourhood, though, to judge from the enormous numbers grazing about, one would think a few might well be spared, especially as they are never killed or knowingly sold by the natives for food.

Our camp had been pitched on either side of a dry nullah, whose banks were covered with bamboo clumps and various shrubs. The Nawab and his friends were on the left, whilst our three tents were on the right bank, and in the dry bed of the river, which becomes a swift and dangerous stream during the rains, we had our kitchen, stables, and servants' quarters.

Our tents were shaded by two large mewah-trees,* then covered with a mass of sweet-smelling flowers, and the ground was strewed with their fallen blossoms. The natives collect them each day, for, when fermented, they produce an intoxicating liquor. Bears are particularly fond of the mewah flower, and are nearly always to be found in their neighbourhood. They are also a favourite food of birds, and always at daybreak and sunset flights of beautiful green pigeons and little, crimson-headed paraquettes pay them a visit, and, having feasted, fly off again.

The jungle close by was very thick, and had many fine trees, whilst the bushes and shrubs were of all varieties, clumps of bamboos, waving their graceful tops in the breeze, adding, as they do every-

* Mewah is the Hindostani word for fruit, but I found that the natives always called this particular tree by that name.

where in India, to the charm of the landscape. The horses were tethered in the nullah behind us; the elephants and camels formed a little camp of their own, whilst the bullock-bandies made a zereba at the back of us. Altogether, with these and the numerous groups of camp-followers round their fires, busy cooking rice, the scene was very picturesque.

During breakfast, our head shikari, a small, wiry-looking man about sixty years of age, called Kishtia, came in, and a group of eager faces was soon formed round him to hear the news. He reported that he had tied up sixteen bullocks the night before, in various parts of the jungle, but there had been no kill, so there was nothing to be done that day. He knew of four tigers close by, amongst which was a man-eater, and he had no doubt that, with patience, we should bag some, if not all, of them.

For the benefit of the uninitiated, I will here give a short account of the way in which tiger-shooting is managed in this part of India. When it has been decided to shoot in a certain district, the shikari are sent out some weeks or even months beforehand to get khabar,* or information as to the number and habits of tigers about the different villages, and also to study the best means of circumventing them.

Once a shikari has taken up a district for his masters, it is not etiquette for anyone else to shoot in that part during the same time. This is a very sensible rule; for, were it otherwise, sport would be spoilt by different parties colliding. In our case Kishtia had been sent out in December, and, being one of the most reliable and experienced shikaris in the Nizam's territories, he seemed to know each tiger for miles round as well as a porter recognises the members of his club. On arriving in the neighbourhood of known animals, the shikari gets a certain number of cattle from the villagers, and these he ties up at night to stakes at intervals in the jungle haunted by the tigers. They are sup-

* Khabar, signifying news or information, is pronounced khuber.

plied with grass and water, and made, as it were, comfortable, but they always seem to know what they are put there for, and generally bellow loudly on being left. Next morning at daybreak, the shikari visits the different baits, or 'cool-ghars,' as they are called. Should one have been killed, he approaches it very stealthily, not to disturb the tiger, but he follows the track, and makes quite certain as to the whereabouts of the beast, who, after his meal, will lie up and sleep in a shady place, if possible near water. The tiger always kills the bullock in the same manner, *viz.*, by a blow on the spine close to the neck, after which he sucks the blood, and then eats the hind-quarters.

The shikari, having made sure of the whereabouts of his quarry, returns to the village, secures two or three hundred beaters, and comes into camp with his news. Then, in the heat of the day, when the tiger is generally asleep, the sportsmen proceed to the ground. In some parts it is most difficult to procure bullocks to tie up as coolghars, for they are the sacred animals of the Hindoos, who do not like them to be killed; but, when this was the case, we could always get buffaloes, about which they are not so particular, and paid a rupee for each one tied up. When one was killed by the tiger, the price was five rupees, not an extravagant sum according to English ideas.

There was great excitement waiting for Kishtia's arrival in camp of a morning, and the culminating point was reached when we heard from him the words, 'Gharra hua,' 'There has been a kill,' whereas deep depression stole over us at the announcement, 'Gharra nay,' 'There is no kill,' as that generally meant an idle day in camp and broiling in our tents. We soon learnt to know what the news would be, by watching Kishtia's step in the distance as he approached the camp; for, if he had good news, he walked with an elastic tread, very different from his slow, dejected gait when there was no kill. Besides wanting to show us sport, it was a matter of considerable moment to him, for we always gave him the government reward, which is twenty-five rupees for a tiger, fifteen for a panther, and five for a bear, and he generally got ten rupees from the gun lucky enough to bag the beast.

On our first day, having no kill, there was no alternative but to lie in our tents. The heat was tremendous, and, our luggage being on the backs of coolies, we did not get it until the afternoon, so in consequence were somewhat uncomfortable. At last they arrived, and at five o'clock we dressed and walked up the nullah, with our guns, in search of small game for the pot; but in this we were not successful, for, although we heard many pea and jungle-fowl about, we did not get a shot, and, the darkness coming on, we returned to camp and squirted, with carbolic, some specimens of small birds we had shot.

That and every succeeding night we slept in our beds just outside the tents, with loaded guns beside us, in case of midnight prowlers. This was a very primitive place; the inhabitants had seen few white men, and the day before our arrival had nearly all left the village in fear of us, and were only just beginning to return to their homes.

Next morning I was awoke at daybreak by hearing the green pigeons flying for food into the branches of the trees above me, and, taking up my gun, I soon shot several. Their plumage is beautiful, and they are excellent eating. As the Nawab and all his followers are strict Mussulmen, I had to keep one of the men by me to cut each bird's throat as it fell; this he did whilst uttering a short prayer. Without this ceremony, which is called 'Hallal,' no Mahometan would touch the game, and many a time have I cursed this custom, when a rare specimen I have wished to preserve has been brought to me with the throat cut from ear to ear, and thus completely spoilt. The sound of my shots soon awoke the rest of the party, who joined in the sport; but it did not last long, for the pigeons' feeding-time never exceeded half-an-hour, after which they flew away and disappeared, until the time came round for their evening meal.

I dressed quickly, and, having got hold of one of the village shikari to carry my rifle and show me the way, went for a walk in the jungle with my shot-gun in search of peacock. My shikari saw a good many as he crept along, but they were always too sharp for me. I find it is the invariable experience of sportsmen that the peacock is one of the hardest things to approach. When beating for tigers, and therefore unable to fire, they would often fly so near that I could have knocked them over with a walking-stick, but I never had any luck when going deliberately after them. Of course, in Rajpootana, where they are sacred and therefore unmolested, they are to be seen feeding about like tame door-fowls; but in the Deccan they are as sharp and cunning as hawks in England. The Nawab also went out this morning and shot a very fine hornbill, which I should have much liked to preserve, but, alas! it had been hallaled, and therefore quite spoilt as a specimen.

On my way back to camp, I came across the fresh track of a tiger, which my shikari assured me had passed but a few minutes before, so I hurried back for fear of disturbing him, but to-day again 'no kill' was reported, so we had to get through the long hot hours as best we could, reading, writing, drawing, and sleeping.

After breakfast, some Rohillas came into camp with tame performing bears and a three-quarter-grown tiger, secured by five ropes attached to a collar and dragged along by five men. The poor brute looked harmless enough, and proved to be so, for, wishing to see how a tiger attacked a bullock, the Nawab bought one, and had the tiger led up to it, when, instead of its attacking the ox, the tables were reversed, for the latter put down its head and went at the tiger with its horns, whilst the monarch of the forest beat a swift retreat behind his keepers. The Nawab now got out his photographic apparatus and did a picture of the tiger and another of our party in camp.

This evening I again strolled out with my gun to shoot some small birds for preserving. I had a walk of four or five miles and was returning in the dusk, when about a hundred yards from camp I suddenly heard a fearful roar close by me, followed by a scream from a monkey. Looking in the direction of the noise, which was in the nullah to my right, I saw the trees full of chattering monkeys, and took in the situation. A tiger or panther had succeeded in catching one of them and was lying close beneath the trees with his victim. I had two Mead's explosive shells in my pocket; I changed them quickly for the shot in my gun and stepped into the nullah, but, the darkness having set in, I could see nothing, so returned to camp. On telling my tale I was assured that I had done a very risky thing, for a panther, which it turned out to be, disturbed at his food, especially at night, is a most dangerous beast, and, as I had been within a very few paces of him, it was a wonder he had not sprung at me. We all took our rifles and returned to the spot. The monkeys were still chattering, and we could hear the panther growling in a bamboo clump four or five yards off, but it was pitch dark, and therefore too dangerous to advance, so we reluctantly left him to his supper and returned to camp.

The next evening I had a curious adventure in connection with this panther which, whilst on the subject, I may mention. I had been out all day after small game, and at six o'clock in the evening was returning to camp very hungry, not having tasted food since early morning. Under these circumstances one's interior is apt to feel put out and to utter groans and pleading appeals for help. I had just shot a lovely little bird which I wished to skin. It fell into the nullah close to the spot where I had heard the panther the night before. There was a rather steep descent to this place, and I was sliding down it, when I heard a deep growl quite close to me. I cocked my gun and sat quite still, every moment expecting the animal to spring upon me. It was a short period of intense excitement, but still nothing stirred. Suddenly the thought flashed through my mind, could it be that it was only an internal appeal such as I have alluded to? This was possible, but not being certain, and thinking discretion, &c., I scrambled up the bank, abandoned my bird, and hurried into camp, only to be greeted with derisive laughter when I told my story.

The report soon spread amongst the natives that we had a doctor in camp, and in consequence Lauder's tent was besieged every morning by a crowd of the halt and the lame, and all manner of diseased. It was an interesting sight to see him sitting in his cane-chair, with a large box of medicine before him, and to observe with what faith they all went off with their doses, some being strong enough for a horse; but then a native is not satisfied unless he gets something he can feel.

We had been having very bad luck, as far as our tiger-shooting was concerned. We knew as a fact there were several about within a mile of

THE START FOR A TIGER BEAT

our camp, and could see their fresh puds each day as we walked into the jungle, and yet they would not look at our coolghars, the fact being that, there were so many deer and other game about, they got quite enough to eat without. Two of our baits had been killed, but they had fallen victims to a panther and hyæna respectively, so their lives had been thrown away.

A good shikari can always tell what animal has killed the bullock, both by the pud marks and by the way in which it has been destroyed, as each one seems to have its own peculiar method.

We were getting rather down on our luck, having now been three days without any real khabar. At last Kishtia came in to say that, although none of our bullocks had been taken, a tiger had killed one of the village cows and dragged the carcase into the jungle about two miles from our camp. He added that he was positive there were five if not six tigers about. The shikari was busy all the early morning collecting the villagers to act as beaters, and at half-past eleven the camp presented a very animated appearance. About two hundred men were squatted in a semi-circle, nearly naked, armed with sticks, rattles, tomtoms, and squibs, and some had old match-locks, with fusees a foot long. In the centre of this circle were the five elephants being loaded with rifles, chargals,* and the various things necessary for shooting. The Nawab's tonga, to which two lovely pure white oxen were harnessed, was also there, as well as four or five horses, for those who preferred going to cover in that way instead of on the backs of elephants.

The bandobast being completed, we left the camp in a long line at twelve o'clock, the Nawab and myself in the tonga and the others on the horses. On reaching the jungle side, we each of us mounted our elephants, the beaters were sent round, and, guided by Kishtia, we proceeded through the forest to our stands. The jungle was very thick, and one had to keep a sharp look-out to avoid the branches of the trees. It was

* Skin bottles containing drinking water.

most important to be as quiet as possible, and no talking above a whisper was allowed; but the branches at times made a fearful row by scraping against the iron howdahs, and then Kishtia would look round with disgust and alarm depicted on his swarthy countenance.

It had been arranged amongst us that we should take it in turns to go into the best place. I being the eldest of the party was told off for that honour to-day, and my elephant was halted close to a large tree, with a clear place in front where the tiger was likely to show himself. The other elephants were posted in similar places about fifty yards apart. After waiting patiently for an hour, the first tomtom sounded and the beat commenced. I was intensely excited, and strained my eyes for the first glimpse of the lord of the forest. As the beat approached, the noise was quite awful: tomtoms, rattles, crackers, gun-shots, and shrieks combined, sounded as if all the devils from hell were loose. Still no tiger appeared; and at last Kishtia came up in front of the beaters in a most dejected state to say that the animal was not in the beat, his (Kishtia's) theory being that the noise made by the branches scraping against the howdahs had frightened the beast away. We had another beat with no better result, and returned to camp at four o'clock very much disappointed. We amused ourselves till dark shooting green pigeons.

One hears a great deal in India about the ravages of snakes, and with good reason too when it is considered that their bites cause the deaths, on an average, of about twenty thousand people yearly. The Government pay a very good reward for any cobras, kyrites, or other venomous snakes that are killed; but the Hindoos are by their religion so averse from taking life, that they will generally merely step out of the way of one of these deadly creatures, instead of killing it, so that the number of snakes in India increases rather than diminishes. Although I lived in districts where they abound, and where I heard of them almost daily, I must confess I saw but few.

The Indian snake-charmer is a wonderful conjuror,—for a conjuror he certainly is. One day at Poona, when I was lunching with the Duke and Duchess of Connaught, one of these men appeared in the compound. He declared that the place was full of snakes, and so it turned out; but I think he must have brought them with him. Anyhow, the way he did it was most marvellous. He was in a state of nature, except for a small waist-cloth, and this I examined to see that it contained no snakes. He stood up in front of the verandah, which was covered with creepers, and began to play on a reed instrument, at the same time peering sharply into the foliage; all of a sudden he would make a spring forward and pull out a snake. Close to my tent he caught a very large cobra in this way, seizing it by the back of the neck as it lay under a stone, and showing us the fangs, which he afterwards extracted with a knife and stick. If he had placed it there, it was a marvellous feat of legerdemain, and yet the most credulous amongst us could scarcely believe that the compound was such a preserve for reptiles. He produced them from all corners of the garden. After he left, we saw no more of them.

That evening I had a curious adventure. I was sleeping in a tent close to the spot where the cobra had been taken, and had just got into bed, when I felt a strange kind of waving movement between the two mattresses under me. I at once jumped to the conclusion that it was a snake, and so getting up in my bed I stamped as hard as I could on the mattress, by way of killing it; then all being still I lay down. I was just dozing off, when again I felt the same undulating motion, so getting up I lit my candle, got my stick, pushed the mosquito-net aside, and prepared to investigate the matter with my left hand, whilst with my right I grasped the stick ready to strike. No sooner had I raised the corner of the mattress than a huge rat jumped out, and afforded me some fine sport, but eventually got away. However, I was greatly relieved to find it was not a cobra, as I had expected.

It is very dangerous in the hot weather to go about one's bath-room with bare feet, for snakes are apt to crawl into cool and damp places out of the great heat. Major Creagh told me that he once found a kyrite wound round his washing-basin, and only saw it just in time, for in another moment he would have placed his hands on it, and a bite from one of this species means certain death in five or ten minutes.

I never but once saw a man who had recovered from the bite of a cobra, and this was an officer whom I met in Káthiáwár. He had just come in from playing tennis, and was examining the grass brought in by the grass-cutters for his horses. They always place it in small heaps, and it is necessary to examine it thoroughly in order to see no soil is mixed with it. My friend thrust his hand into one of these heaps, when it was laid hold of by a cobra and severely bitten. He described his feelings to me as very awful, and was convinced in his own mind that his fate was sealed. However, without a moment's hesitation he bound up his arm as tightly as possible above the place and plunged it into nearly boiling water, which took off the skin. A doctor, now arriving, cauterized the wound, an agonising operation, and made him drink a whole bottle of brandy. When, as very soon happened, he became drowsy, four sepoys were told off to keep him awake and walking about. He was quite sensible, and knew that sleep meant death, yet the longing for it was so great that he was constantly imploring them to let him lie down. He had fearful pains all up his arm and down the side of his body, which lasted several days; but at length it subsided, and after six months he felt as well as ever. This was a wonderful recovery, and the only way he accounts for it is that the cobra must have bitten some animal a short time before, and thus got rid of part of its venom.

One hears endless horrible tales of snakes in

India, but I have to thank my good luck that I never had any adventures with them myself.

The language spoken all about this part of India is Telagu, and Hindostani is very little understood amongst the village people, so that in many places we should have found it difficult to get on with the natives had it not been for an Englishman, who was in the Nawab's service, and who spoke Telagu as well if not better than his own language, as he had never been in England since he was a baby in arms.

CHAPTER VIII.

PAGET ARRIVES—FLYING FOXES—CHANGE CAMP—LINGUMPAH—NATIVES ARRIVE WITH A GRIEVANCE—FIRST SIGHT OF A TIGER—GHARRA HUA—TIGER'S ESCORT—FUTILE BEAT—BEARS—ANECDOTE—ELEPHANTS DISCARDED—TIGER BEAT—PAGET SHOOTS FIRST TIGER—TOMASHA FOR DEAD TIGRESS—SKINNING TIGRESS—LODER SITS IN A MACHAM—PIG-STICKING EXTRAORDINARY, AND SEQUEL—GHARRA HUA AGAIN—TIGER HEADED BY NAWAB—PAGET KILLS SECOND TIGER—KING-FISHERS.

CHAPTER VIII.

Our bad luck continued for some days; the tigers seemed determined not to take our 'bails.' The shikari came in one morning to say that two of the 'bails' (bullocks) had been killed, but by panthers, and that there were a great many tiger puds about, so we organised two beats, hoping to come across something, but again we were disappointed, and then determined to move our camp as soon as Colonel Paget arrived. This he did on the afternoon of the 9th. He had had a long ride, but looked very well, and gave us some interesting details of the Burmah campaign, where he had been attached to the mounted infantry.

On the morning of the 18th I was up at half-past four, and was surprised to see the trees above me full of flying-foxes, instead of green pigeons. It was still dark, and they continued feasting until daybreak. Herbert and I rode off ahead of the rest of our party to our new camp at half-past five. We had only fifteen miles to go, but it was very pleasant. The first part was through a dried-up jungle, reminding me forcibly of an English covert in winter; but as we approached the village of Lingumpah the scenery underwent a thorough change, and we came across green fields, cultivation, and lastly a jungle composed of bamboo clumps and various shrubs and trees scattered about, with broad paths intersecting it, giving one the idea of vistas in botanical gardens.

On arrival we discovered that the man in charge of the tents had pitched the camp very badly. The Nawab's tents and the cooking arrangements were all together on a piece of marshy ground surrounded by paddy fields, whilst ours was nearly a mile off, and with a ploughed field between us.

Being very hungry after our ride, we breakfasted at once, after which the Nawab ordered his tents to be struck, and moved close to ours under the shade of a huge banyan-tree, so big that it covered three large tents with its branches. While we were having our smoke, a man and his wife came in with a regular 'ewe lamb' story. They went down on their knees before the Nawab and complained that his shikari had forcibly taken their only buffalo and tied it up as bait for a tiger. The Nawab told them they should be well paid for it, but this did not seem to console them at all, and they were sent away in great distress of mind. Later on Kishtia came in to say that there was no kill, so I am in hopes these poor creatures recovered their pet.

As usual, when no kill, we had an idle day. Paget and Lauder developed a great capacity for sleep, and were in a state of unconsciousness nearly the whole time, and much annoyed when now and then I looked in and inquired after their health.

Towards evening I took my gun and strolled through the jungle. Just as I turned the sharp angle of a nullah, I came face to face with a tiger standing not ten yards from me. Having only No. 8 shot in my gun, I fumbled in my pockets for some bullets, but before I could get them out the beast had seen me and disappeared in the dense jungle.

Next day we were cheered with the news, 'Gharra hua.' It seems that one of our bails* had been killed within half-a-mile of our camp, and close to the spot where I had seen the tiger the evening before. After the usual preparations, we started off at twelve o'clock, and passed the dead buffalo with the marks of the tiger's teeth in its throat and the whole of the hind quarters eaten, so he must have had a good appetite. A shikari, who had been on the watch, came up here and said that he had tracked the tiger to a hill about three miles off. The jungle was very thick,

* Hindostani for bull, or bullock.

and it was hard work making our way through it on the elephants, for, unless continually on the look-out, one was liable to decapitation from the branches which spread out in dense masses about the height of our heads. Besides this, our great object was to prevent branches scraping against the sides of the howdahs. In this we were decidedly unsuccessful, for so great was the noise made by our progress that when we got into our places, and before the beat began, we heard the growls of the langoor monkeys, a sure sign that the tiger was on the move. He managed to sneak out of the beat without our getting a shot at him.

It is curious the way in which the big langoor monkeys always accompany a tiger and give notice of his approach, and it must be annoying to him to be continually accompanied by this noisy suite. They are generally to be found in large flocks, some run in front of him, some at his side, and others jump from tree to tree above him, all the while uttering a sound something between a bark and a growl. The tiger occasionally has his revenge on an over-rash member of this family by despatching it with one blow of his powerful fore arm.

We went off to another rocky hill full of caves known to contain bears, but, although we threw in a number of squibs and hand grenades, we could not induce Bruin to show himself.

The Indian bear is a very shy animal, and seldom found out in the daytime, except quite early in the morning, when returning from his nightly prowl, or again in the evening when leaving home, but is rarely to be seen during the heat of the day. He will always attack when prevented from entering his cave, but on going out will try to run past his molesters.

A friend of mine, a great Indian shikari, told me of a curious adventure he had with bears. He was walking through the jungle in early morning when he came across two. He fired at the first and wounded it, and then gave his second barrel to the other one. They both went on and were tracked by the blood to a cave in the side of a hill. My friend felt confident that he had hit both of them, but the natives were of a different opinion, declaring that the first was hard hit and would certainly die in a few minutes, but that the second, not being touched, would quit the cave very soon after he discovered that his companion was dead. Such being the case, it was best to leave them for the present and to return after breakfast in an hour's time. This was done, but the coolies still refused to enter the cave to haul out the dead bear, so my friend, having placed a pistol in his belt and lighted a torch, went in himself, with one of the men's lungís, or turbans, in his hand, intending to put it round the dead animal and drag it out. Sure enough he soon found the body and was busy at his work, when, in the gloom, his hand came in contact with warm fur heaving under the pressure, which clearly proved that it was a living animal. In spite of the torch, the darkness was so great that he could not make out which was the head and which the tail of the beast, but putting his pistol quite close to the side he fired. No sooner had he done so than a huge bear got up and came at him. He was standing with his back to the entrance of the cave, and all he could do was to shove the lighted torch in the bear's face. Twice he did this, repelling his foe each time, but on the third occasion Master Bruin knocked him over and bolted out of the cave without doing him any further injury. The appearance of the bear outside was, however, greeted by a volley of shots from the natives, the bullets splashing on the rock a few inches from my friend, and being much more dangerous to him than the bear's claws. Eventually both animals were bagged and taken to camp.

On the 13th of March, Kishtia came in with the ever welcome news that a tiger had killed a bullock within a mile of camp, and, having eaten the greater part of his victim, was lying up close by. Most of the party were so disgusted by their numerous disappointments when mounted on elephants that they resolved to discard them, and to sit on trees. The Nawab and myself, however, determined to give hati * another trial, especially as we were told that the covert was not very thick.

It was a beautiful piece of jungle, looking more like a private shrubbery than a wild forest. The Nawab and his elephant were placed close to a dry nullah on the right of the line, well concealed by bamboo clumps. I came next about fifty yards to his left, whilst Arthur Paget was in a tree forty yards to my left, and the other guns at similar intervals further on. No sooner had we all got to our places than the tomtoms of the beaters began to sound, and five minutes afterwards the Nawab fired a double shot into the jungle followed by the cry of 'Sachmie sher!' ('Wounded tiger.') This warning is very necessary to enable the beaters to get up trees and out of the way of the infuriated beast. We kept very still as the beat was some way off, and presently

* Hindostani for elephant.

I heard the langoor monkeys coming in my direction. A rush through the grass to my left caused me to look round just in time to see Arthur Paget bowl over a fine tigress within twenty yards of me. If he had missed, I should have had a splendid shot, as she was making straight for me; but he killed her very cleverly, having hit her close behind the shoulder with a bullet out of his ·450 Empress, which knocked her completely over. She crawled about twenty yards, and on going up to the spot on my elephant I found her stone dead under a tree. The beaters now came up, but on the news spreading that another tiger and a wounded one also was about, they climbed up the nearest trees, and looked like so many chattering monkeys. Dr. Lauder, having brought out his camera, now did two pictures of us round the dead tigress, after which we organised a beat for the one seen by the Nawab, but in vain, and we returned to camp at two o'clock.

The dead tigress was put on a pad elephant,

TOMASHA BRINGING IN DEAD TIGRESS

and the march back was a curious sight, all the villagers turning out. They and the beaters carrying branches of trees surrounded the elephant bearing the beast, and dancing in front of it, with their tomtoms playing and amidst hideous yells, brought it into camp. The Nawab photographed and I sketched this scene: we then went off to see the tigress skinned.

It is very necessary to watch this process, or the natives are apt to carry off the whiskers and claws, both of which are considered potent charms. A tiger has also two small bones embedded in the flesh of the chest and disconnected with all other bones, which the natives will invariably carry off, if they can. The fat, too, is used by them as a specific against rheumatism, and in these parts some of the lowest castes will eat the flesh of the tiger, as, in fact, of any animal they can get.

We cut open the body and examined the wound. The bullet was split up into small pieces, and had completely shattered the lungs.

That night, there being a fine moon, Loder had a macham or platform of boughs, built in a tree overlooking a piece of water, and sat up all night in hopes of getting a shot at some beast coming to drink, but he saw nothing; and, from all I could glean from the Indian shikaris I have spoken to on the subject, this plan is seldom successful, so I never tried it myself.

If there is one thing more than another which makes my blood boil it is wanton cruelty to animals. One morning the young Nawab was very anxious to try his hand at pig-sticking; as there were no wild pigs handy, he procured a village boar, and riding after him with a spear proceeded to stick him. The poor beast got two fearful wounds, and was making off, pelted and otherwise ill-treated by the natives, whilst the Nawab came to breakfast rather pleased with himself. I could not stand the sight, and calling to Paget, who had a revolver with him, we went off together to put the poor creature out of its misery. The plucky animal, although so seriously wounded, no sooner saw Paget approach than he turned round and charged, giving him barely time to put a bullet into his head, which killed him at once. As the boar had really large tusks, it might have been no joke had the bullet not taken effect.

Another kill was reported early on the 15th of March. It was about five miles off this time, and entailed a hot ride in the middle of the day; but it was my turn for first place, so I was all excitement. The jungle on the way was full of magnificent tamarind-trees. I plucked the fruit as I went along, and found it most refreshing, as it is acid and astringent.

I had a capital place in the beat close to a dry nullah, with an open place in front of me, where the tiger would probably break covert. I was on an elephant, with Lauder in the howdah behind me. Soon we heard the sound of the tomtoms and guns. A beautiful civet cat was the first thing to appear, running close under my elephant; he was soon followed by numerous jungle fowls and peacock, some of which I could almost have touched with my rifle; then I saw some langoor monkeys, sure sign that the tiger was not far off. They kept streaming past me fifty or sixty at a time. I cocked my rifle and redoubled my attention, when to my disgust the Nawab came straight in front of me on his elephant. This was fearfully annoying just as I was expecting a shot. I whistled to him, but the din made by the beaters was so great, he could not hear me. His elephant kept on moving, and I knew he would head the tiger back. Just then I heard a terrific roar, and sure enough there was the tiger, which would have come out close to me, rushing back through the beaters.

I never felt so disappointed in my life, but I am bound to say that no one could have been more sorry for what had happened than the Nawab himself. It seems that the beaters having come up and passed the place where he was stationed, he fancied the beat was over, and came on. I was hidden from his sight by a clump of trees. So vexed was he with himself at having spoilt my sport, though, as it turned out, it was a very pardonable mistake, that he went straight home.

But my bad luck was not to end here. We started for another beat in the direction the tiger had taken, the shikari saying that he had eaten so much of the bullock that he could not go far. We took up our positions again, but this time no power on earth would keep my elephant quiet. He whisked his trunk about, groaned, and kept changing his feet, so that it would have been almost impossible to get a steady shot. The mahout dug the iron spike he carried into his head until it was a mass of gore, but with no effect. Lauder, who was behind me, and has very keen sight, saw the tiger in the jungle just in front of me about to break, when noticing my elephant he went off to the left, and broke under a tree in which Paget was seated. The latter soon despatched him, the first bullet passing through the stomach, the second through the spine, whilst a third in the heart put him out of his suffering. I was very glad that we had bagged another tiger, but much disgusted at my individual bad luck. It was a curious fact that Paget should kill the only two tigers he had come across, and that I should have seen both shot within twenty yards of me without being able to fire.

Whilst in this camp I saw several of those beautiful many-coloured king-fishers (Omnicolor Halcyon), and procured a very good specimen, which I regret to say was afterwards destroyed by white ants.

CHAPTER IX.

MOVE TO JULUMPAH—A FINE-LOOKING JUNGLE—TRACKS OF GAME—HUNT HERONS WITH HAWKS—COOLING SODA-WATER—SHOOT JUNGLE-FOWL—ALL GUNS IN TREES SAVE MYSELF—PET MONKEY—THE MOTHER FOLLOWS US—LAUDER MISSES THROUGH CRAMPED POSITION IN TREE—SICK CHILD—GREAT DAY'S SPORT—MAN WOUNDED BY TIGER—ELEPHANT BOLTS—NARROW ESCAPE—THE TALK AT DINNER.

CHAPTER IX.

I WAS not sorry when it was decided that we were to change camp and move on eight miles to a place called Julumpah. I had met with such bad luck in this last camp that I hated the very recollection of the place. Our new one was pitched in the midst of a fine mango tope, with a large tank close by, the banks of which were covered with storks and herons. As 'no kill' was reported, the Nawab had out his falcons, and it was very pretty to see them go for the white herons, and to watch the manœuvres of the latter to avoid their enemy. When tired, the herons would perch amongst the mango-trees, taking care to have some protecting branches above them. The weather was getting hotter each day, and now the thermometer in our tents registered one hundred and two degrees at mid-day. The heat made one very thirsty, so that the pop of the soda-water-bottle was to be heard at all hours of the day. Having no ice, we cooled our drink by placing the bottles into an empty crate and covering them with straw; the crate was hung by ropes to the largest branch of a tree, and water poured over it at intervals, whilst a native swung it backward and forward by another rope. Sometimes the swinger would go to sleep or neglect his work, but the next customer for a drink invariably found him out by the temperature of the liquid, and would visit his wrath on the body of the delinquent.

There was a very fine-looking jungle here, and some distance from the place, where we tied up for tigers; so, as there was no fear of disturbing these beasts, we therefore organised a beat for small game in this other direction, and went off about half-past three in order to shoot in the cool of the evening. No doubt there was lots of game about, as we saw numerous tracks of sambur, chetal, or spotted deer, and bear, but the beat was badly managed, and all the animals broke back. The only chetal that came forward broke under Ismael Khan's tree, and he missed him. A fine wild boar also passed close to Paget; he could not, however, get a shot. Luckily a lot of jungle-fowl had got into a nullah, and, surrounding this, we had a nice hot corner of rocketting jungle murgi,* one bag being eighteen jungle-fowl, one peacock, five hares, and a few quail. I worked very hard skinning some of the best specimens when I got into camp.

Some of the men had caught two young monkeys, and the Nawab made me a present of one. Pat, as I called him in honour of the day (the 17th of March) on which he was caught, was quite a baby, and I made a great pet of him. I put a collar on him and attached him by a rope to a box full of straw close to my bed, but was disturbed all night by the mother-monkey calling in the trees above to her offspring. She must

* Hindostani for fowls.

have come at least ten miles after her infant, which had been caught that distance from camp the day before. He was what nurses call very 'fractious,' and gave me a great deal of trouble for the first two or three days.

At Dr. Lauder's morning dispensary here, a curious and horrible case was brought in. It was that of a little girl about six months old, with a tumour the size of a cocoa-nut growing out of her spine. There was no cure for it, but Dr. Lauder offered to pay the father all his expenses if he would take the child to the Hyderabad Hospital; this, however, he refused to do, so the poor little thing must linger on until death releases her. She was a bright-eyed, interesting-looking child, and seemed free from pain. She gave me much more the idea of a European child of three years old than an infant of six months.

Now at last I have to chronicle one of the best and most exciting day's sport that it will probably ever be my good fortune to witness.

On the morning of the 19th of March, Kishtia

came in at nine o'clock to say that a tiger had killed a buffalo tied up about two miles from camp in the middle of the jungle. We made our preparations and started off on ponies about twelve o'clock. On getting to the place we found a very dense piece of dried-up jungle, with large white smooth-barked trees scattered about it, and in front of us a small rocky hill full of caves. Flocks of vultures and hawks were hovering above our heads, indicating by their movements the place where the dead buffalo lay. The tiger had dragged his prey part way up the hill, and then eaten nearly the whole of it.

All the guns, except myself, were to be in trees. I was on one of the Nizam's elephants, which had the character of being a very staunch beast, and from whose back many a tiger had been shot.

It was Herbert's turn for first place, so he climbed into a well-placed white tree, commanding a full view of the hill in front. Loder had second place to Herbert's left, and was close to the

N 2

gharra, or dead beast. Paget was on a tree on Herbert's right. I came next to him on my elephant, and Lauder was in a tree beyond me again. Lauder and I were virtually out of the beat, and did not expect to see anything of the sport.

It was two o'clock before the first tomtom sounded; but hardly three minutes later I heard a tiger's roar to my right, followed by a shot from Lauder's rifle. I stood at the ready position, straining my eyes through the jungle for fully twenty minutes, when again I heard a roar to my right, and through the dense undergrowth could just make out part of a tiger, trying to break out quietly between Lauder and myself. He was from seventy to eighty yards off, and there was a mass of trees and shrubs between us, so that I had little chance of killing him; but I fired so as to turn him to Lauder. In this I was successful, for I heard his shot; but, as I learned afterwards, poor Lauder was so cramped up in his tree that, although the tiger came and stood close to him, he could not take proper aim and missed entirely.

In the meanwhile I heard four or five shots to my left in Herbert's direction, and wondered what it could mean, as the tiger was on our side. Kishtia soon came up and asked me to go on my elephant to Herbert's help. I did so, and found him still sitting on his tree, in great glee, having shot two tigers, whilst Loder had killed a panther. I took Herbert up into my howdah, and we soon found his first animal lying stone-dead, shot through the heart. We were all looking at it, and the beaters were coming down the brow of the hill in front of us, when we were startled by a fearful roar in that direction, and turned round just in time to see a tiger rush out of a cave, seize a man, and roll over a rock with him. It was a terrible moment, and made me feel quite sick, but to our intense relief the man got up and the tiger left him, and bolted into another cave. All the beaters were up trees in a second, and looked like so many langoor monkeys, chattering in mortal terror. Lauder had now joined us in the howdah, and we took the elephant to a place about thirty yards from the cave containing the tiger, and where I got a clear view. Kishtia and all the shikari stood on the rock above it, and called Paget to them. He had only two cartridges, and shouted to his boy John to bring his second rifle and some more ammunition, but John was safely up a tree one hundred yards away, and, whether he heard his master or not, held fast to his safe position, and Paget had to do without him.

The shikari lit some squibs and rockets, and threw them into the cave. The tiger roared, showed part of his head for a second, and bolted back again. Kishtia now, with the greatest pluck, crawled down to the mouth, lighted some straw and flung it in. Some fell outside, and soon the whole of that part of the hill was a-blaze. The trees crackled, and the smoke and heat were terrific. Presently the tiger rushed out roaring, and Paget and Kishtia both firing at the same time, the brute rolled dead in the flames. I made sure that from where I stood I should have had a shot, but my bad luck still pursued me, for the tiger had bolted out of a side hole.

Having secured the body from the flames, we now went off on the elephant in search of the other wounded animals. A number of vultures were sitting on a tree, and, knowing they would not remain there for nothing, we steered through some dense jungle, getting our faces much scratched by the thorny creepers, and under a tree we found a beautiful panther stone-dead.

The only thing now was to get Herbert's second tiger. Kishtia and another shikari searched every blade of grass, and at last came upon blood. It was a beautiful sight to see them tracking it through the densest bushes. Sometimes they were at fault, but invariably got on the trail again, although it was so faint that an inexperienced eye could detect nothing. We on the elephant followed them with our guns ready to give the wounded tiger a warm reception should he come out and charge us. In this way we went on for four or five hundred yards; our progress was slow, the sun was sinking low in the sky, and we seemed to be getting no nearer our quarry. Kishtia came back to say that we should have to give it up, as the darkness coming on made it dangerous business; but he felt sure we should find the tiger in the morning.

The words were hardly out of his mouth when a native shouted, 'Sher! Sher!' ('Tiger! Tiger!') We were just then in a most awkward place, passing under a tree with a big branch, which threatened to decapitate me, on a level with my chin. I had cleared it partly away, when I saw a huge tiger bounding towards us, with open mouth, eyes dilated with rage, ears back, and tail in the air. It was a magnificent but terrifying sight, for our men were scattered about on the ground around us, and an accident seemed inevitable. Kishtia rolled under an ant-hill, and the tiger cleared him at a bound without seeing him, his whole attention being concentrated on

BESET BY PERILS

our elephant. He was now not ten yards from us, and we were about to fire when the elephant trumpeted, turned suddenly round, and bolted as fast as he could lay legs to the ground. The tiger was close to us, and I felt sure that in two more bounds he would be upon us, and drag Lauder out of the howdah. We were rendered utterly helpless by the branches, which knocked the guns out of our hands as we tried to get them up. At last, in a clearer spot, I was bringing my rifle to my shoulder, when a branch knocked me over. Herbert was luckier, and had just time to let off his rifle before he was knocked down. He had made a beautiful shot, bowling the tiger right over. Still the elephant went on, and every moment we expected the howdah to be smashed and its occupants killed by the branches. The mahout behaved capitally, and, though severely wounded and cut about, he stuck to his work, and by dint of hammering the elephant's head with his iron spike at last stopped him. I had often heard of the danger of an elephant's bolting, but never realised the awful horror of such a catastrophe. The moments seemed like hours.

We brought the elephant back and found the tiger, or rather tigress, in her last gasps. Herbert's final shot had gone through her mouth to her brain. How we all congratulated each other on our escape! Now the danger was past, we felt it was well worth undergoing for the excitement. We had encountered all the dangers of tiger-shooting to-day: a man mauled, a charging tiger, and a bolting elephant. We quickly hoisted the dead tiger on the elephant and made for camp.

It was a glorious bag, and one rarely exceeded; three tigers and a panther. As we rode back in the dark, the hill was lit up by a mass of flame, and the sky all aglow with the lurid glare. We had surely destroyed a stronghold, and were delighted with our day's work, the more so when we learned that these identical tigers had killed no fewer than twelve men during the last rains.

The villagers ought to have been grateful, but, if they were, they kept it to themselves.

The wounded man was now brought in on a charpoy. He was one of the shikari, and a very useful and plucky young fellow. His leg had five teeth-marks in it, two of which were an inch and a half deep, and yet he did not make the slightest fuss. He told us that the tiger had made for his throat, but that he had beaten it off with his gun, and had then been seized by the leg. Dr. Lauder syringed the wounds with carbolic acid diluted with one hundred parts of water. It must have been a painful operation, but the man never winced. We got up a good subscription for him, and collected enough to make him rich, according to his own humble ideas, for many a long day to come.

At dinner that night the talk was of nothing but tigers. We assisted till a late hour at the skinning of the beasts by torchlight. None of the party, I think, are ever likely to forget the 19th of March, 1887.

CHAPTER X.

IDLE DAY IN CAMP—MOVE CAMP—JUNGLE PLANTS—BIRDS—DAK ARRIVES —ENGLISH LETTERS—PALMS PLANTED IN OTHER TREES—GHARRA HUA—I SHOOT A BEAR—CURIOUS BONE—GYMKANA IN CAMP—DUCK-SHOOTING—FEAR OF NATIVES—CAMP MOVED TO PENGUDPAH—JUNGLES FIRED—TODDY PALMS—PAGET NEARLY SHOT BY ME—SUDDEN STORM—WHITE ANTS—SKILL OF INDIAN COOKS—MOVE CAMP TO PALONCHA—LODER'S BOY MEETS A BEAR—BAD LUCK—ENGLISH MAIL—GHARRA—MORE BAD LUCK—HERBERT LEAVES US —PANTHER IN CAMP.

CHAPTER X.

Next day there was 'no kill,' a fact we did not regret, for the shikari wanted a rest from their hard work of the day before. They had been given as usual, after a good day's sport, a goat or two and a bottle of whisky; but, although told to take a holiday, little wiry Kishtia could not keep still. He had an idea that the tiger I had shot at yesterday might have been hit, and was not satisfied until he had scoured the jungle for some miles round the place, but, finding no signs of blood, he gave up the pursuit.

The camp was rendered somewhat disagreeable by the smell of the dead tigers' bodies; they were, however, made short work of by hundreds of vultures, and we amused ourselves firing at the birds with our rifles at long ranges, rather to the danger of the surrounding villages. So thoroughly had we disturbed this district with noise and the jungle fire that it was determined to move on, and on the morning of the 21st we struck camp at half-past five, and rode off to Sellnacunda, about fifteen miles off. It was a lovely ride, and, as usual, Herbert and I got in ahead of the party. The camp was again pitched under a mango tope, being both cool and shady. The jungle here was very green, a fact that made it appeal more to our sense of the beautiful than to sport, for where there is verdure there is plenty of water, and in such districts it is difficult to find the tigers, as they are not obliged to return to the same places to drink.

I strolled into the jungle, and noticed a good many trees and shrubs hitherto unknown to me, and several orchids; there were also numbers of birds with brilliant plumage flitting about, a pleasant change after the everlasting 'Tom! tom! tom!' of the coppersmith-bird and the 'We feel it!' of the hot-weather, or brain-fever bird, as it is called. This latter's call is most peculiar. It begins by 'We feel it!' in low notes, and repeats these sounds three or four times each in a higher key, until at last it is drawled out to a high 'We-ee-e-e feel it!' Besides these two birds, I must mention the Indian plover, which flies about when disturbed uttering, 'Did he do it!' as distinctly as a human being.

The excitement of the day in our new camp was that of receiving letters by a camel dâk, or post. After being for some weeks out of the world, we read our letters with avidity, and devoured the contents of newspapers six weeks old. None of us received any bad news, so there was not the slightest cloud to mar our enjoyment.

I noticed one peculiarity about the trees in these parts, which is, that the natives are very fond of planting the seed of the cocoa-nut and toddy-palm into the heart of another kind of tree. The palm grows and flourishes at the expense of the parent tree, which invariably looks sickly and delicate; but it is a curious sight to see these tall palms jutting out and waving their heads thirty feet above the foliage of the tree it grows from.

On the 22nd, a sowar rode to camp at eight o'clock in the morning with the news that there had been a 'gharra,' or kill, six miles off, and that two tigers had been seen. The Nawab had a slight attack of fever, so he and Dr. Lauder stayed in camp, whilst the rest of us rode off at eleven.

It was excessively hot, but the jungle was lovely with the numerous creepers hanging from the trees, the flowering shrubs, and the gay-plumaged birds.

After going five miles, we met Kishtia coming to tell us that the tigress and her cubs, who had killed one bullock, had gone right away after their breakfast, and that it was no use beating for them; but he added, there were some 'bearish' looking hills a mile or two off, so we decided to have a beat there.

I was posted on the Nawab's favourite elephant

on the left of the line, close to a ledge of rock leading from one small hill to the other. Soon after the beginning of the beat, I heard the dead leaves crackling in front of me, and, looking in the direction from whence the sound proceeded, I saw a huge black bear about thirty yards off apparently coming straight to me. He would have given me a splendid shot, but just then my elephant saw him too, and, trumpeting loudly, wheeled completely round. This was exasperating. The bear, hearing the noise, looked up, gave a grunt, and went off to the right. I had only just time to fire at him with my ·500 Holland Express: he gave another grunt and rolled on his head, but in a second was up again and disappeared towards the other guns, where he was received with a succession of shots and eventually expired close under the tree in which Herbert was sitting. We examined him carefully, but could only find one bullet-hole just behind the shoulder, and, as we traced the blood from the place where I had rolled him over, he was undoubtedly mine; but it is wonderful to think how he could have gone off at all with a wound right through his lungs.

That evening I superintended the skinning, and was still more surprised when I saw the havoc made by the bullet which had traversed both lungs. He was a very large bear of the kind, being six feet long by three in height. The natives are fond of bear's-meat, and numbers of them came and dipped rags in the blood, which is considered a cure for convulsions amongst children.

The bear also possesses a bone which is much in request amongst the natives, its supposed value being that the owner of it will be blest with a numerous family. As soon as a bear is killed, it is surrounded by an eager crowd anxious to get hold of this bone. Knowing this, I put my servant on guard, and told him on no account to lose it. He brought it in to me next day, saying there were great heart-burnings over it, for they said, 'The Burra* saib' (as they called me) 'has a large family, so he cannot require the bone.' I offered

* Burra means big or old.

to lend it to them to stir up their rice, but this I heard was of no use unless they actually owned the bone, and that I would not give up.

By way of a little change, we organised a gymkana in camp, and arranged a long list of events, some of which, owing to the darkness, did not come off. One meeting began with tent-pegging, and, as Mahomet Ismael Khan is one of the champions of India at this feat, it was very interesting. There seemed to be no way of puzzling him, for, riding at a gallop at the small bamboo pegs, his lance never missed its mark; we tried split pegs and also putting them sideways, but always with the same result. Herbert also was very good at this. We placed small onions on posts about ten yards apart; Ismael Khan rode full speed past them, sword in hand, and, although it was then nearly dark and the onions not much larger than filberts, he never missed cutting one of them in two.

Our sports ended by hanging up the carcase of a goat, riding past it at a gallop, and cutting it in two with a sword; at this exercise, one of the most difficult for a novice, Mahomet Ismael Khan was again undefeated. The night had now come upon us, so we returned to our tents and got ready for dinner.

The tigers in this particular district seemed very shy, and we had to content ourselves for the most part with small-game shooting. There was a tank six or seven miles off which afforded us good sport with duck and snipe. We shot several kinds of the former, viz., the great Indian grey duck, pintail, whistling teal, and common teal. All are good eating except the first, which is coarse and fishy. The inhabitants of the village close to the tank came out in force to stare at us, most of them never having seen a sahib before. I went up to one boy to examine a silver ornament round his neck, but he ran away screaming as if in dread of his life. This state of things will soon come to an end, for the railway is fast approaching, and in another thirty or forty years all the novelty and charm of India will be at an end, when the country will be full of hotels and overrun by Cook's tourists and *hoc genus omnia.*

Pengudpah, eight miles off, was our next camp. Never shall I forget the heat of that ride, although taken in the early morning. A hot wind was blowing, the jungle was very dry, and a large tract of it was on fire. The natives fire the jungle at this time of year, in different parts, as it much improves the quality of the grass which comes up with the June rains, but at the same time it is an extravagant method of manuring, for many valuable and beautiful trees are annually destroyed in this way. Often looking out of my tent at night have I seen a whole hill-side ablaze, and much animal and insect life must be thus destroyed.

We were thankful to see masses of toddy-palms about Pengudpah. What meant toddy to the natives was bread to us, for we used the toddy instead of yeast, and when we could not get it we had to subsist on stale bread and biscuits.

Many tigers were reported about here, but there was no kill, and again we went duck-shooting on a large tank close to camp. We managed to get eighteen or twenty, although we lost many more in the thick rushes and weeds; but it was ample for the pot, and after mutton chops and tough chicken they proved a welcome change.

What might have been a nasty accident, happened to-day. My servant gave me my cartridge-bag with what I supposed to be all shot cartridges, and I loaded my gun without examining them. Paget and I were at opposite sides of the tank, about three hundred yards apart. There were a great many duck on the water, and in order to put them up I told Paget I would fire at them aiming towards him. My astonishment and horror may be imagined when, on firing, I heard the ping of a bullet which ricocheting from the water went within a couple of feet of Paget. He took it very coolly, merely shouting out, 'Please don't do that again.' But it made me feel horribly uncomfortable.

At Pengudpah I had my first experience of an Indian storm. It had been oppressively hot all day; at four o'clock we were drinking tea under Lauder's tent when, suddenly, we heard the sound of distant thunder. In another five minutes it was rolling all round us, and suddenly a terrific whirlwind encircled us. The tents began to shake. Some of us clung on to the poles, whilst others made for the ropes, but all in vain, for so strong was the wind that the whole tent soon collapsed burying us in the ruins. Luckily no one was much hurt, and as soon as we could scramble out we made for the other tents which were threatening to follow the example of the first. As it was, hats, clothes, papers, and books were flying all about the ground, but in less than half-an-hour the tempest was over and the sun shining again as if nothing had happened. The ground was strewed with green mangoes torn from the trees by the force of the wind, and every chair and table was covered with white ants. These are veritable pests in India, for they destroy everything they can get at, and kill the finest trees in the jungle. The fine mango tope we were under was rapidly succumbing to them; the natives never attempt to put a stop to these ravages. Sometimes I have seen them in thousands coming up my tent ropes, and would place some carbolic acid at the upper end when they would skedaddle as fast as possible.

We had an example, after the storm to-day, of the skill of Indian cooks in difficulties under which a European would generally collapse. All the fires had been put out, the cooking-tent blown down, and the whole place covered with dust, yet at the usual hour we had a most excellent dinner of soup, fish, mutton cutlets, poulets sautés, curry, and asparagus: not, I think, a bad bill of fare under the circumstances.

We were rather tired of Pengudpah, and much to Kishtia's disgust determined to move on to Paloncha. Kishtia maintained that we were wrong, and asserted that he knew of lots of tigers about, and that if we would only have patience we should get them. Our time, however, was limited: Herbert had to be back at Poona on duty the beginning of April, and we were all anxious to push on to the river Godaverry, of whose beauties we had heard so much. We sent on most of the servants at night, and followed as usual in the early morning, reaching our destination after a charming ride of about twelve miles. This was the prettiest camp of the whole expedition, and that is saying a great deal. The tents were pitched under giant mango-trees, and we were surrounded by a lovely jungle, toddy-palms, and a large grass máidan.

On arriving, we were told marvellous tales of the amount of game in the neighbourhood. They knew of fifty tigers, whilst the sambur and chetal were so thick that they jostled each other in the jungle. But by this time we knew that native accounts must be taken 'cum grano.' Loder's servant told us a wonderful tale of how a bear had come up to him in the jungle during the night and frightened him considerably; this same boy was about the ugliest specimen of humanity I had ever cast eyes on, and I should say that one look of his would be enough to frighten any bear in Hindostan.

We tied up eighteen beasts the first night, but, in spite of the fifty tigers, none were killed. Kishtia declared that a tiger had come at one of them, but that the bullock had resisted him successfully. How we cursed that bullock!

During a walk through the jungle we saw any amount of tiger puds, and began to grow hopeful. We organised a beat for other game, but with our usual bad luck, for two bear and a quantity of jungli buckri (a small antelope with four horns) broke back through the beaters without giving us a shot. The heat was greater to-day than I have ever felt it; so we were glad to return to camp, but later, getting into the two tongas, we drove off to a tank a couple of miles distant, and shot some wild duck and sand-grouse for dinner. An English mail in the evening somewhat consoled us for the failure of the day.

The news of a gharra next morning took us out again. The heat was terrific, and the jungle so thick that no elephants could go through it. Of this I was glad, for I had begun to lose faith in them for tiger-shooting as practised in the Deccan. I had what is called a machan, or seat made with crossed boughs, rigged up for me in a tree about twenty feet from the ground. The beat began at one o'clock and lasted till three, but we saw nothing. It turned out afterwards that a tigress with two cubs was in the beat, but, the ground being very steep and rocky, the beaters did not keep a good line, and the tiger broke back through them. Tiger-shooting at the best of times requires a good deal of patience, and the sportsman must be prepared for numberless disappointments; but we felt we had certainly now had more than our share of both, and looked forward eagerly for the turning-point in our luck.

Herbert, having received orders that he was to rejoin His Royal Highness the Commander-in-Chief, whose aide-de-camp he was, left us to-day. It is always rather sad to break up a pleasant party, but in this case it was doubly so, for he was so cheery, his spirits so unflagging under trials and disappointments, that we felt rather down in our luck as he rode out of camp at two o'clock. He had a long and tiring journey before him, a ride of sixty miles through the jungle to rail head, and then a jolt in a construction train to Warungal, where he would get into the regular train for Hyderabad.

That evening we again shot over our tank with success, whilst Mohamet Ismael Khan, the young Nawab, and other native gentlemen, had a beat in the jungle. They saw quantities of chetal, jungli buckri, and pig, but although they fired ten shots between them, did not hit a thing.

In the middle of the night, whilst sleeping outside my tent, I was awakened by a noise, and saw a dog rushing through the camp as hard as he could lay legs to the ground. Next morning I was told that a panther had been after him and had passed close to my bed.

CHAPTER XI.

LUCK CONSIDERED WITH REGARD TO SPORT—GREAT QUANTITIES OF BANDAH MONKEYS—BUDDRACHELLUM WITH ITS SACRED TEMPLES—NUX VOMICA TREES—MOVE TO BAGGUMALPAH—FIRST SIGHT OF GODAVERRY—GREAT STORM—NATIVES COLLECTING TODDY—VISIT BUDDRACHELLUM—FISH FOR MUGGAR—TAKE RIVER TO HUMWARUM—KHABAR—THE NAWAB'S TOILETTE—GYMKANA—BLACK BUCK SHOOTING—I SHOOT BLACK BUCK FROM THE TRAIN IN KATHIAWAR—NAWAB KILLS BIG TIGER—SHOOT MUGGAR.

CHAPTER XI.

Up to this time my record, as regards tiger-shooting, has been one almost entirely of failure, principally owing to sheer bad luck. Sport generally entails vicissitudes of fortune, and it is this very uncertainty that makes the blood flow quicker through the veins and lends its great excitement to the chase; but a continual run of bad luck such as we had experienced is very disheartening. We had but a limited time before us, and were anxious to make the most of it, so that each successive blank day was harder to bear. Kishtia urged us to have patience and remain where we were, but of course he could not understand our desire to see and do as much as possible in a short time. We had heard glowing accounts of the river Godaverry, which had been described as a sort of sporting Eldorado, and we wished to push on, so after our failure with the tigress and cubs it was settled that we should go on the next day. Kishtia had good khabar of some tigers at a place called Nagaramat eight miles off, and we eventually came to a compromise by agreeing to halt there, instead of pushing on straight to the river.

During the ride between these two camps, I came across great quantities of Bandah monkeys, and in an open máidan some eighty or a hundred of all sizes were congregated together. I set spurs to my horse and rode after them. Such a comical sight as they presented I never before witnessed. The big male monkeys trotted off ahead, stopping and looking round every now and then, whilst the females, with young ones clinging to them, brought up the rear. As soon as they reached the jungle, they scrambled up the trees, and looked down with an expression of tranquil security.

Our camp, though under mango-trees, was in a dusty plain close to a huge nullah, and no sooner had we breakfasted than complaints were lodged as to the quality of the water. Lauder made a thorough investigation, and found that nearly all the trees round us were nux vomica, the roots of which penetrated into the water supply and rendered it highly dangerous. Under these circumstances, we made up our minds to strike camp and to move on eight miles to Baggumalpah on the banks of the river Godaverry. This move, made in the heat of the day, was a real scorcher. Most of the horses were tired after the morning ride, so several of us drove in the tongas.

What with the heat and jolting, I was very glad when we got to our destination, a large plantation of toddy-palms on a cliff looking down on the river Godaverry. This being the dry season, there was but little water, and a large stretch of sand five hundred yards wide, lay on each side of the stream, which during the rains and some months after them is covered with water. On the bank just opposite to us, and which is British territory in the Madras Presidency, is the sacred town of Buddrachellum with its temples. Pilgrims visit it from all parts of India, and just at this time a fair and festival were going on. Crowds of natives were crossing the river all day, and the town was then said to contain twelve thousand pilgrims.

We had not been more than an hour in camp, and the Nawab's was the only tent pitched, when the wind suddenly got up and in a very few minutes increased to a perfect hurricane. Never did I see such dust. During the fifteen minutes that it lasted, the air was black and we were covered from head to foot with a thick coating of dust. We were almost suffocated, and hid in corners for shelter.

As soon as the wind ceased, the rain came down in torrents, drenching us through and through and turning the dust on us into mud. After half-an-hour was over the storm subsided, and the sun came out again, but the camp was flooded and we were occupied for some time in digging trenches to carry off the water. In spite of these adverse circumstances, we again sat down to a most excellent dinner provided by the wonderful Said Cassem.

I never saw so many parrots as there were in this camp. Towards sunset they kept flying in, in hundreds, and we shot a good many for practice, as flying high in the air, with a twist, they are by no means easy to hit. The pests of this place were the white ants which had been disturbed by the rain, and spread themselves over the ground, on our clothes, and in our beds, and hardly gave us a moment's peace till I had saturated my tent with carbolic acid.

Sleeping outside my tent, I woke next morning at daybreak, and was interested in watching the men come round and collect the toddy from the palm-trees. Toddy is made from the sap of the tree. The tops of the flowering sprouts are cut off and chatties* tied round them, the sap, which would naturally run through to nourish the fruit,

* Earthenware bowls.

thus falls into the chattie, and is collected each morning and fermented. The men climb up the tall smooth stems of the tree, with the help of a fibre girdle, and hang the different chatties, as they remove them, to their waists.

After 'chota hazri,' we started for a visit to Buddrachellum on the opposite bank. We walked over the sands to the bed of the river, then, mounting elephants, rode across the stream, which though rapid is only about five feet deep in the ford. It was a curious sight: five elephants, an escort of sowars, and a large following on foot. As soon as we reached the opposite bank, we were met by a band composed of tomtoms and flutes, the latter shrieking out discordant notes and blown with all the might of the players. The streets were crowded, and we rode through the bazaar to the temple, where, seated in a low durbar-room, the Nawab had to listen to a long address and petition in Telagu. The sacred jewels were brought out for our inspection, but there was nothing worthy of remark amongst

MUGGER FISHING IN THE GODAVERRY

them, so, after the usual ceremony of attar and pan,* we were glad to mount our elephants again, and to return to breakfast.

In the afternoon we drove to a part of the river, about a mile from camp, to see the natives fish for muggar, or alligators, with nets. It is a curious sight, and, when one considers what a dangerous animal a muggar is in the water, one feels it to be an occupation requiring a great deal of pluck and nerve, yet the men and boys brought up to it seem to think nothing of the risk they run. The muggar fishermen have wonderfully sharp sight, and could make out muggars in the water when we could see nothing. As soon as they have spotted one, they jump and frighten him into a corner of the bank, by beating the water and poking at him with bamboo poles, whilst at the same time they shout at the top of their voices. Having got him into a handy place, they bring out a

* This is a custom all over India, and consists in placing a wreath of flowers round each visitor's neck, a leaf full of betel-nut in his hand, and a few drops of attar of roses on his handkerchief. Often some bottles of attar of roses are given as well to the departing guest.

large-mesh net and gradually draw it closer in towards the muggar, who at first retires to the hollow of the bank, and under the roots of trees, but he is soon poked out, when, in trying to rush off, he gets entangled in the net, and is drawn on shore. I noticed that the men take good care to jump quickly aside when he makes his final rush, as he would snap off their legs with a single bite of his huge jaws. We caught three muggar, the biggest being ten feet long; a very large one got under the net and away.

We spent two very pleasant days here, but as time was getting short, and we wished to make up our game-bag, we settled to leave on the 2nd of April for Humwarum, fourteen miles further down the river. By way of a change, we hired two native boats, and, having seen all the bullock bandies and boys off by road, proceeded on our journey by water. It was an excessively hot day, but these boats are provided with awnings made of maize and toddy-palm leaves, so that we were not exposed to the fierce rays of the sun, and

FLOATING DOWN THF RIVER GODAVERRY

amused ourselves shooting ducks, waders, and different kinds of water birds as we floated down-stream. The scenery reminded me very much of the Nile, especially the large sand-banks in the middle of the river, covered with birds of all descriptions. At three o'clock we espied our horses and camels on the bank, and, having brought the boats to, landed and rode to camp, which was barely half-a-mile off, in a mango tope at the edge of a jungle which looked decidedly tigerish. Kishtia soon came up with the news that he had seen one close to camp.

Next morning, whilst lying in bed, I watched the Nawab at his toilette, and was very much amused to see that he had ten men waiting on him: a man for each boot, one for his brush and comb, one holding a glass, another a towel, and so on. It is true Eastern custom for a great man to have all these followers, and he is never left alone for a second—servants told off to supply every single thing he can wish, even a man to tell him stories to send him to sleep at night.

By way of amusement for the servants and camp-followers, we got up another gymkana, and hundreds of the villagers came to see and to join in the sport. The first event was an obstacle race, in which they had to jump over and crawl under hurdles and tent sheeting, ending up with a small barrel with both ends out, through which they had to crawl. Though barely big enough for one man, they would make for it two or three at a time, and got jammed in the middle, so that it was a wonder none of them were seriously injured. This was followed by elephant and camel-races, the meeting winding up with a menagerie race, or animals, each driven by a different man, and included sambur, chetal, a wild cat, a dog, a donkey, fowl, frog, and monkey, and was won by the latter, driven by the Nawab. At our various camps, presents of live animals had been made to the Nawab, so by this time he had a large collection round his tent, and the young deer of different sorts had become quite tame, and would follow their keepers anywhere.

There were some black buck about here, and Paget was up before daybreak trying to stalk them, but in vain. They are very shy, and when much disturbed almost impossible to approach. I had had some very good black-buck shooting at Indore in January. Captain Norman Franks, the commissioner there, took me out one morning into the Maharajah Holkar's preserves, and on a large plain we once saw quite a thousand buck in different herds. They were very shy, but we got at them by driving quietly about the plain in a native bullock tonga, and, when within a hundred and fifty yards of them, I would slip out with my rifle, and, resting on one knee, get a quick shot, whilst the tonga still moved on, and before they had time to notice me. In this way we killed five fine buck, and came home to breakfast.

When travelling in Káthiáwár in the train, between Wadwan and Vankaneer, I saw large herds of black buck scattered over the plain through which the railway runs, and, having asked the engine-driver to give me notice if a herd was crossing the line by blowing his whistle twice, I managed to get a shot or two, and knocked over a fine buck with my rifle whilst the train was going at full speed. The buck was sent back for from the next station and bagged. The venison is excellent, and I know few dishes to come up to black-buck neck cutlets.

Kishtia came in next day to say that a tiger had killed one of our bullocks within two miles of our camp. Paget had first place to-day, and was posted in a tree beside a nullah, the Nawab in a machan on the opposite bank, and I next him on his left. The beat began at two, and was nearly over when I heard the now well-known roar of a tiger, followed by two cracks from the Nawab's rifle, and a shout announcing that the beast was dead. He proved to be an enormous tiger, with the largest forearm I have ever seen, and measuring nine feet six inches. The doctor got out his camera and photographed him as he lay in the nullah. Later on, when he was skinned, we found an old wound with the bullet still in it, and some of the villagers seem to have had an intimate acquaintance with him.

During the evening, I strolled down to the banks of the river, rifle in hand, and had a shot at a large muggar, as he lay floating in the water, with his back just above the surface. He sank to the shot, and I could never ascertain whether I had hit him or not. It is almost impossible to get the body of a muggar killed in the water, as they invariably sink to the bottom at once, and this I found the case when shooting at crocodiles on the Nile; but, whether one gets these animals or not, it is always some satisfaction to think that the world may contain one less of these dangerous brutes.

CHAPTER XII.

WANT OF VEGETABLES—SETTLE TO MOVE TO PENGUDPAH—LONG RIDE—LOSE OUR WAY—GREAT THIRST—AN AWFUL FIX—JUNGLE SEEMED INTERMINABLE—ARRIVE AT PENGUDPAH—GREAT DAY'S SPORT—FIVE TIGERS BAGGED—MAN KILLED BY TIGRESS—I AM GIVEN A HORNBILL—NATIVE RAILWAY MAGISTRATE—HIS VIEW OF AFFAIRS IN THE DECCAN—DOLLY—CHETAL SHOT—LEAVE PENGUDPAH—BIRDS—ARRIVE AT SEMALPAH.

CHAPTER XII.

One thing we felt the want of, and missed dreadfully in the jungle, was a supply of fresh fruit and vegetables, these, to us, necessaries, being almost totally unknown in India at any distance from large cities. The natives seem quite contented as long as they can get their rice, and the only thing in the shape of vegetables which they cultivate to any extent is the chilli. At some places we got bringals, a sort of egg-plant, but they were very few and far between, so that the only green food we could rely on was in tins, and we soon got heartily sick of 'cotelettes *à la* tinned Gardiner's wife.' Buggallumpah was the only town where we got plantains, and, although these were anything but good, we devoured them eagerly, such is the want felt for fresh fruit.

We now held a grand council of war as to our future plans. It was the 5th of April, and we had to be back in Hyderabad by the 18th at the latest, so that the time was very short. The two questions before us were whether to break fresh ground or to return to Pengudpah, where, although we had not seen a tiger, Kishtia seemed confident we should have good sport. So confident, indeed, was he about it, and so strongly did he urge the matter, that we finally settled on this latter place. Pengudpah was at least thirty, if not thirty-five, miles from our camp, and it was a case of sending off all our things at once, and making up our minds to a long ride the next day; however, this we regarded lightly, and we were all ready for a start and on our horses at 4.30 a.m. on the 6th of April.

Knowing we had a long and hot ride before us, I had put a soda-water-bottle full of cold tea, and a few biscuits in a haversack, which I slung round my shoulders. The Nawab had told us the night before that the road had been chumaned as usual, but after the first half-mile we were quite at fault and could see no white stones; however, some natives whom we came across put us on a track with the stones clearly marked out. Most of our party went on quickly ahead, but Lauder and I followed at a gentle amble, for which these horses are so famous. By some negligence on the part of my boy, my bottle of tea had not been properly corked, and with the jogging of the horses the stopper came out altogether, drenching me; but of this I did not so much care as for the loss of the drink, for, as the sun was getting very powerful, I felt I should soon require some refreshment.

At a quarter-past eight, having ridden, as we supposed, about sixteen miles, we were again at fault, and were, moreover, much surprised to see Paget and Loder riding back towards us. Our disgust may be imagined when we discovered that all this time we had been riding on the back trail laid down from our last camp. We had not discovered our mistake before this, for we came by river the last day and therefore did not recognise the country; but now, there sure enough was the grove of toddy palms not half-a-mile off, and on the opposite bank the temple of Buddrachellum.

Our faces fell, for we were in an awful fix. Our horses were tired, the sun was scorching, and we were just as far from camp as when we started in the morning. Moreover, the track was not marked, and our only way of getting to Lingumpallah, fourteen miles off, and where our change of horses were waiting for us, was by hiring a native to show us the way, and following him at foot's pace.

Never shall I forget the heat of that march. My throat was so parched that for my bottle of cold tea I would have given its weight in gold. My horse was so done that he nearly came down on his nose three times, and the only way I could keep him going at all was by digging him with my spurs. The jungle seemed interminable. Passing along mile after mile through these dried-up trees and bushes, fearfully damaged by white ants, the dried leaves crackling underfoot, and a blazing sun overhead, reminded me very forcibly of one of Gustav Doré's weird pictures.

At last, about half-past eleven, we saw a large clump of toddy-palms, and we met several buffalo in the jungle, both sure signs that we were nearing some village. Digging our jaded beasts with our spurs, we were soon at Lingumpallah. My tongue clove to the roof of my mouth, and I could not speak. Some Brahmins brought us milk, but it was boiling hot, and they would not let us drink out of the chatty, so we were in despair.

Just then it struck me to ask them whether they had seen anything of our horses, and we got the joyful news that the Nawab was breakfasting under a mango tope not two hundred yards off, and that the horses were all there too. Never shall I forget the delight of finding milk, soda-water, and fresh limes. We poured down the liquid in buckets-full before we could speak, and then explained the mistake we had made. The Nawab had not left camp till two hours after us, and had enjoyed his breakfast under the shade of the tope at the end of an easy ride, and could afford to laugh at our misfortunes.

But we still had sixteen miles before us, so we could not waste much time. I got on a favourite Arab called 'Humdum,' who at first was very fresh, but the heat was so great that he soon caved in, and towards the end of the ride first came down on his nose, and then went through the disagreeable performance of stumbling with his hind legs. However, at one o'clock we got safely to the camp at Pengudpah, and after more drink we got off our things, tubbed, and lay down in our tents till five, when taking up our guns we paid a visit to our old tank, and shot a quantity of wild duck and teal for dinner.

And now I come to an account of the most successful day's sport of the expedition, though, unfortunately, a melancholy accident robbed it of a good deal of its pleasure.

On the morning of Thursday, the 7th of April, Kishtia came in to report a 'Gharra,' and added that, as nearly the whole animal was eaten, he thought that there must be more than one tiger in the place.

We had great difficulty in collecting beaters, as the villagers were very shy, but, by pressing in the services of the bandy-wallahs* and other camp followers, we mustered one hundred and twenty men. These were not many, but we supplemented them by sending all the elephants into the beat. We left the camp at half-past twelve, and rode through three miles of jungle before coming to our places, which were near a dry nullah, and with a fine clear space in front, through which the animal could be easily seen. The Nawab and Loder were to be in a large machan in the same tree at the left of the line; but, after two or three unsuccessful

* Drivers of the bullock-carts.

attempts, the Nawab gave it up, as the tree was too high for him, and went to one nearly behind me. I, having first place, was in a good tree fifty yards to Loder's right, whilst Paget was the same distance to my right, and Lauder again beyond him.

I had been an hour-and-a-quarter in my tree, had drank nearly the whole of my chargul of water, and was nearly driven wild by the small bees which settled about me, and tickled me dreadfully, when I heard the first tom-tom. This brought me to attention, and a very few minutes afterwards a tiger came out about one hundred and twenty yards to my left front. I made sure he would come straight to me, but something startled him, and he entered some thick bushes, making towards Paget. I gave him both barrels of my ·500 Express; but I must have gone over him, for he never stopped, but, going straight for Paget's tree, was despatched by him when not six yards off. No sooner was this over, than I saw another tiger coming towards me. I fired, and this time he stopped dead

UP A TREE

short, and gave a 'whuff! whuff!' sure sign that he was hit. However, he seemed soon to recover, and, turning towards Paget, halted midway between us, looking at the former. I was very awkwardly situated for shooting in his direction, and was just getting my legs round for a shot, when Paget fired, and sent him into the nullah behind, where he seemed to receive a warm reception from the Nawab and his party, who gave him three shots between them.

Again I turned to my front, and saw a tiger coming within thirty yards of me. I fired and knocked him over. I could see I had broken his spine, and he looked up at me with a terrible grin on his face. I gave him another shot with my ten bore, and killed him. I had barely time to load, when still again another tiger came on. I fired a snap shot, and hit him in the back near the tail. He bled profusely, but went on towards Paget, who fired two shots without stopping him; and I saw him disappear in the nullah, when the Nawab again shot. Paget now got a shot at a fifth tiger, which I did not see, and soon after the beaters came up.

With the help of an elephant, I got out of my tree. We ought now all to have assembled, sent the beaters into trees, and walked up in line to the wounded tigers, whose whereabouts, with the help of the elephants, we should have soon discovered; but, to our dismay, just at this moment we heard a rifle shot, followed by a tiger's roar, and found that the Nawab had gone on on his elephant, independently, after a wounded tiger. This was a dangerous proceeding; for all the men were about, and the enraged beast would be sure to attack the first man he could lay hold of.

Everyone was alarmed, and, sure enough, we had not long to wait, for just then a shikari ran towards us saying that a wounded tigress had killed one of the men. Walking carefully, with our rifles at full cock, we went to the spot and there found the poor wretch, who was a body-servant of the Nawab's, not dead but fearfully wounded. His scalp was nearly torn off and hanging over his face, he had a huge bite in the neck, and a very bad wound in the arm, which exposed the biceps. We made him get up and walk to the elephants; he was quite sensible, and got into one of the howdahs, which took him off at once to camp. The tigress had gone on, but, after four or five more shots from the Nawab, was despatched, and we found her stone dead under a tree. The other tiger was dead in the nullah, so that we had now bagged all five. The shikari declared that there was a sixth tiger in the beat, but none of us saw anything of him.

In tiger-shooting whoever draws first blood claims the animal. I had therefore got three, and Paget two of those killed to-day.

We laid out the five tigers close to the spot where they had been killed, and Lauder took a photograph of us with our game, which proved to be a tigress and four full-grown cubs.

We rode back to camp and went to see Lauder dress the poor man's wounds. He was a fearful sight, but bore the pain without flinching, Lauder told me that eight out of ten Europeans would die at once under the circumstances, but he has great faith in a native subject owing to the very healthy life they lead and from the fact that they take no stimulants and eat very little meat, thereby keeping their blood cool.

Next morning, early, Lauder and I went over to see how he was. The people who had sat up with him said he had passed a very bad night, and was continually getting up and imagining that he was wrestling with the tiger. At the time we went in to see him he was unconscious, but his pulse was very strong. However, an hour afterwards Lauder was again sent for, and returned to tell me that the poor fellow was dead. The shock to his system must have been tremendous, and he seems to have gone out suddenly at the end. He, it seems, has no one to blame but himself; he had been warned that it was simply madness to follow the track of a wounded tiger, but he would listen to no one, and wished to show the Nawab how keen he was.

This tragic circumstance threw a complete gloom over the camp, but the natives never waste much time in grieving. At twelve o'clock he was buried, and after that no one seemed to think anything more about it.

The Nawab made me the present of a live Hornbill which had been brought into camp. The poor thing had had an eye poked out, but otherwise was in perfect health. I sent for a lot of jungle fruit, which it ate freely. It was certainly a most uncanny bird to look at, but soon got tame.

One of the native railway magistrates came in to pay his respects to the Nawab, and was invited to stay with us for a few days. He was an intelligent man, speaking English fluently, having served the British government in the North-West Provinces for some years before entering the Nizam's service. I was very glad to have a talk with him on the state of the native population in the

Nizam's dominions. He greatly deplored the state of the country where we were shooting, and told me that the jungle now covers vast tracts of valuable land which used to be in a high state of cultivation and yielding large crops, that there are a great number of old wells and tanks all over the country which, though now dry through neglect, might be restored at a small expense, thereby bringing the country to its former prosperity; for, as I think I mentioned before, water is the only thing required to fertilize any Indian soil. He was a great advocate for peasant proprietorship, and I am of his opinion, for, from what I have observed in my wanderings, a man always takes more pride and pains in what is his own. The Nizam's territories are divided amongst feudal chiefs, of whom the Nawab Vikar Ul Umra is one of the most powerful; we came across large villages and districts belonging to him, and over whose inhabitants he has power of life and death. He is obliged to keep up two regiments at his own expense, one of cavalry and one of infantry, and to pay besides a large sum yearly to retainers and pensioners whom he cannot possibly dismiss, though they are of little or no service to him; therefore, although his income is very large, a great portion of it is spent in this way, and he is unable to make the reforms and improvements which his cultivated and educated mind would suggest.

Whilst I was talking to this official, a number of men came in with a dolly or offering for the Nawab, consisting of a live peacock and a young jungli buckri, or four-horned antelope. These presents were continually arriving, until the Nawab possessed a regular menagerie. This afternoon we inspected all the animals, and found that they consisted of three sambur, seven chetal, or spotted deer, one jungli buckri, one monkey, two muggars, and several jungle-fowl and pea-cock. The muggars were tied by a rope to a tree and continually drenched with water; they looked very unhappy and soon died. The Nawab gave me three of the chetal, which are now all living and doing well at Windsor Castle.

During the afternoon Mahomet Ismael Khan rode into camp in an excited state, having shot a fine buck chetal. It was in the velvet and in good condition, so we dined that night on venison cutlets, which were excellent.

Kishtia came in to say that the villagers had been so terrified by yesterday's fatal accident that even if we had a kill it would be impossible to get beaters, and he therefore advised us to move on. He had been so correct in all his previous advice that we determined to be guided by what he said, and, as he had a great hankering after Semalpah, we settled to strike camp and to move off there the next day.

The Nawab and his followers went on soon after daybreak, but we breakfasted comfortably and started at ten o'clock, my first horse being a bay Arab, called 'Bairam,' very showy, but much more suitable for the parade than the jungle. The ride was decidedly hot, and we were glad to halt half-way, where we changed horses, and had taken the precaution to send on some refreshment.

The jungle scenery was very striking, with its fine trees and clumps of bamboos, and I saw several jungli buckri, hares, and pretty birds. As a rule, although India teams with animal life, nothing is to be seen during the hot hours of the day, but between six and nine o'clock in the morning the whole place seems alive with peacock, jungle-fowl, coppersmith and brain-fever birds, and doves calling, but after that they disappear until the cool of the evening.

We reached Semalpah at half-past three, just a month to the day on which we had left it, and were told by the villagers that thirty-one head of cattle had been taken by tigers since we had been gone. I found my hornbill, which I had sent on, very well, and feeding satisfactorily, and I wasted a good deal of time in watching this solemn-looking bird.

CHAPTER XIII.

IN OUR FIRST CAMP AGAIN—SOWAR RETURNS FROM HERBERT—JUNGLE-FOWL, PARTRIDGES, SPUR-FOWL—LANGOOR MONKEY—PARADISE FLY-CATCHERS—'SOLDIER'S PHEASANT' NOT FIGURED IN GOULD'S 'BIRDS OF ASIA'—GREAT HEAT—GHARRA—TIGER MISSED—TWO GHARRAS—BOTH UNSUCCESSFUL BEATS—ISMAEL KHAN BAGS TWO TIGERS—RIDE TO GALA—HORNBILL DIES—FAREWELL TO KISHTIA—RAILWAY—MONKEY AND DOG—HEAT IN TRAIN—MR. SHEFFER AT MANKOTA—ARRIVE AT WARUNGUL—FORTIFICATIONS—PARSEE OFFICIAL—CARPETS AND CUTLERY—ANILINE DYES—COLONIAL EXHIBITION STIMULATED TRADE—SLEEP IN TRAIN—ARRIVE AT HYDERABAD—GOLD MOHUR TREES—CROWD AT HYDERABAD STATION—DR. AND MRS. LAUDER—LEAVE FOR POONA—CLIMATE OF POONA—LEAVE FOR MAHABLESHWAR—SCENERY ON THE ROAD—PANCHGANNI—PRODUCE—STRAWBERRIES—WANT OF GARDENS IN INDIA—ARRIVE AT MAHABLESHWAR—WOODLAWN—BULBULS.

CHAPTER XIII.

It seemed very odd to be back in the same place in which we had spent so many fruitless days at the beginning of our expedition, and which we had been so eager to leave, never wishing to see it again. The only change we could discover in it since our departure was in the mewah-trees underneath which our tents were pitched. Their sweet flowers had turned to pods, and we looked in vain for green pigeons, or even for the lovely blossom-headed parakeets (Palœorius Rosa) of which I had seen so many on our former visit.

The sowar who had accompanied Herbert on his return to rail head rejoined us here. He reported that, whilst riding through the jungle not far from our present camp, they came across a tiger thirty yards from them. Being both unarmed, they turned their horse's heads before he saw them, and, making a detour, gave the dangerous customer a wide berth; for, although tigers seldom attack people in cold blood, cases of it have been known.

We were up early the morning after our arrival to shoot jungle-fowl and partridges for the pot, and organised a beat down the nullah, which was successful in so far that we got several birds, and some spur-fowl as well. The jungle-fowl of these parts is what is known to naturalists as Sonnerals jungle-fowl, or Gallus Sonnerati, and is quite different from the species found in the Terrai. It is a handsomer bird, and has beautiful hackels, ending with tips which look like yellow wax. These hackels are much prized by salmon fishermen for tying flies, and I brought home a good many. The grey partridge, which is common here, is much like the English bird, but has no horseshoe mark on its breast, and, moreover, it often flies up and settles in trees. I shall never forget how astonished I was the first time I saw a partridge sitting on a branch. The spur-fowl are something between a partridge and a hen of a reddish colour, and are known as the Rufous spur-fowl, or Galloperdix Spadiceus. Some of our beaters caught two young ones about a fortnight old, and the Nawab placed them under a coop with a hen and brood of chickens, but they were very wild and would not feed.

On this occasion we saw several jungli buckri, but, as usual, they broke back, and we did not get a shot.

I was much amused by a big langoor monkey, who came up and sat in a tree not three yards from me without having seen me. At first I remained quite still and watched him; then, making a little noise, he turned round, and, in his alarm at discovering my vicinity, put on so comical an expression that I fairly burst out laughing. These monkeys have beautiful silky coats, and are sometimes shot for them; but I never could bring myself to fire at one. One day, in riding from camp to camp, Ismael Khan came across a large troop of them in an open máidan. He rode for one of the biggest, and, on getting alongside of him, leaned over his horse, seized the monkey by his tail, and swung him completely round. This was no mean feat with his horse going at full speed.

I now for the first time saw the Paradise flycatchers (Muscepeta Paradisi). Their bodies are about two inches, while their tails are fully a foot long, and consist of two feathers. The males are white, with emerald-green heads and crests, whereas the females are of a bronze colour. I thought them the most graceful and lovely birds I had ever seen, and shot two as specimens; but, alas! my No. 2 shot blew them to pieces, and so it was useless trying for any more. But that morning I obtained two fine specimens of the bird vulgarly called the 'soldier's pheasant,' and which is a kind of magpie, with indigo-coloured head and body, with cinnamon wings and tail. It is common all over India, and its deep note was always to be heard in our compound at Poona; but, although I have searched through Gould's 'Birds of Asia,' I cannot find it figured. In fact, I miss a good many common Indian birds, such as the coppersmith, kingcrow, and even the great hornbill, in that work.

The weather was now hotter than ever. We had two thunderstorms, but that did not cool the atmosphere; and it was very trying work sitting all day in our tents with nothing to do. We had brought out a largish stock of light literature, but, owing to the number of blank days, it was pretty nearly exhausted; so we had to devise various methods of getting through the time, such as shooting at marks and vultures with our rifles, and getting up little gymkanas.

At last, after four days, Kishtia reported a 'gharra' in a part of the jungle not more than a mile from camp. We were all in our various trees, I being to the right of the line, where, before the beat had begun, one of the stops close to me sprung his rattle; and this was immediately followed by the roar of a tiger, who, having been disturbed, was sneaking out of the beat. The noise of the rattle turned him towards the Nawab, who, however, missed him, and sent him running on to the young Nawab's tree. Here three shots were fired without effect, and he went off none the worse, but much to our disgust.

There seemed to be a fate against our getting a tiger at Semalpah, and this was still further illustrated by events in the subsequent two days. After our recent bad luck, we resolved to go on to Gala as soon as possible, and so sent on spare tents, luggage, and everything not actually necessary; that is to say, we kept one change of clothes and one rifle apiece, in case of accidents. We were up at six, and just thinking of starting, when a sowar rode in to say that there had been two gharras during the night. One in the same place as the last, and the other six miles off. This changed all our plans. We could not possibly go away with the chance of adding two more tigers to our bag; but the difficulty was to decide how we were to manage the two beats that day. For, although we ourselves could easily do it on horseback, it must be remembered that it takes some time to move three hundred beaters through the jungle.

We held a council of war, and eventually decided to take the far gharra first, come back towards camp to the near one, then, sleeping in our tents for one more night, to leave for Gala next morning at daybreak. All our things having gone on, this involved some discomfort, but we were willing to put up with that for the sake of two more skins.

We started off for our first beat at half-past eight, but had great difficulty in getting beaters. Eventually we reached our trees, and were ready by one o'clock. I never saw so many peacocks as in this beat. They kept streaming out, like pheasants in England when driven to a corner; but, alas! there was no tiger. He had had his meal and gone off.

With as little loss of time as possible, we were again on our horses and made for the other beat. The Nawab was not keen enough to come with us, and he and his following rode straight off to Gala, about thirty miles, where he would find everything comfortable. Ismael Khan also left us on a little expedition of his own to our second camp, which was not five miles from our present position, and later on I had the news that he had bagged two tigers there to his own rifle.

We got to our beat at half-past four. This was much too late in the day to expect sport, but it was worth chancing. I was in a beautiful white tree, perched about twenty feet from the ground, with a clear space all round, in fact it was the very tree from which the Nawab had had his shot two days before, but, alas! nothing came out. It was some time after the beat before they came to me with the ladder, and in the meanwhile I amused myself by carving my name and the date, April 15th, 1887, ''Arry' fashion, on the tree. I wonder if anyone will ever sit in that tree tiger-shooting. It is a beautiful place, and if anyone ever does occupy it, I hope he may have better luck than I did.

We felt very down on our luck on returning to camp. This was our last day's shooting, and we were so much in hopes of ending the expedition with a good bag.

We had a long day before us, so were up at half-past four, and rode through Singarenny to Gala, following our old track. It was melancholy to pass all the land-marks which we remembered nearly two months ago, and to think that our expedition was now at an end. We had expected to get a bigger bag, but still, taken as a whole, we had not done badly; for we had accounted for thirteen tigers, one panther, and a bear, and there is no doubt that if we had had average good luck we should have got from twenty to twenty-five tigers, which was what we expected would have been our number.

At eight o'clock we reached our old camp

under the big mango tope of Gala. The railway had got on a pace during the last seven weeks and was now not half-a-mile off, and a special train was in waiting.

After breakfast, all the shikari came in to say good-bye, and to ask for certificates. We were delighted to give first-rate characters to old Kishtia and his son-in-law, Lucksnia, both most excellent and painstaking men, doing all they knew to show us sport, and never sparing themselves. At eleven o'clock we drove to the station, and found Mr. Molesworth had come down for us. I congratulated him on the progress made in the line, and he told me they were doing all they could to get it to Singarenny, where so much coal was waiting ready to be taken off. This line was only costing in its construction about three thousand pounds per mile, whereas the line to Wadi, though not a bit better made, had through mismanagement cost ten thousand pounds per mile.

My poor hornbill died this morning; of this I

was very sorry, for he had become much tamer and seemed getting reconciled to captivity; but the jolting at night in a small basket on a camel proved fatal to him. I had collected numerous pets in the jungle, but they had all died off except my monkey, which grew tamer every day and was now a very decent size, and afforded great amusement to everyone in camp. The Nawab had a second monkey, which had grown so fond of a big dog that he was quite miserable if taken away from him, and they used always to go about together, the monkey's chains attached to the dog's collar, and the monkey himself riding on the dog's back.

The day was very hot, my glass in the railway-carriage went up to one hundred degrees, but by this time we were so used to heat that it did not distress us much. At Mankota, one of the stations on the line, and the scene of many of Dr. Lauder's shikar feats, Mr. Sheffer, another engineer and a great shikari, came to the station. The night before our arrival he had shot two large panthers right and left, and we went on to his tent, about fifty yards off, to see them. He also showed us the skin of a very large muggar which he had caught in the tank close by, and, on Paget's admiring it, he presented it to him. Further on, at another station, we got out again and had tea with the engineer, arriving eventually at Warungal about five o'clock.

Warungal, the capital of this part of the Deccan, is an interesting old place, and was formerly of great importance. It was very strongly fortified, and the outside lines cover a space of twenty-seven miles, whilst, besides this, there were two inner lines of fortifications.

The head official, a Parsee, speaking English fluently, met us at the station to pay his respects to the Nawab and to see if he could be of any use.

Warungal is now famous for its carpet and cutlery manufactures. A large collection of both was spread out for our inspection near the station. The Nawab presented us each with a carpet, and

I bought one or two more. They are very pretty, but it is a great pity that they use aniline dyes in the manufacture. The colours are very brilliant but never last, and will come off when rubbed with a wet rag; however, the natives are always taken with gaudy-looking things, and thus their sale is insured. This Parsee gentleman, whose name I regret to say I forget, takes a great interest in the progress and prosperity of Warungal, and for that reason has issued an order forbidding the use of these dyes, and imposing a fine when the order is disobeyed. It would be a very good thing were his example followed throughout India, where aniline dyes are so much in vogue. The carpets with fast colours are always known as being 'puckar' ones. The knives, daggers, &c., are well-made, although the steel is not so good as those of English manufacture; but I think Warungal has a great future before it, and, now that the railway is opening out, the whole country trade will rapidly increase.

There is no doubt that the Colonial Exhibition

of 1886 has done a great deal towards stimulating trade and manufactures throughout India, for it brought products of the country to the notice of thousands of people who had never seen them. Labour being cheap, most of these articles can be supplied at very reasonable rates in England, in fact I have frequently seen Indian products offered for sale in London shops for the same price as I was asked for them out there. I feel confident also that the Imperial Institute, when completed, will do a great deal towards this good and important work.

We dined in a tent near the station, and thoroughly enjoyed the luxury of an iced 'peg' after so many days of lukewarm soda-water in the jungle; then returning early to our railway-carriages, which had been shunted to the siding, we turned in for the night.

Next morning saw us all up soon after day-break. The vendors of carpets surrounded the train and did a good trade with the Nawab's suite, who took back many as presents to their families, and, in selecting them, I noticed that they chose those with the brilliant aniline dyes.

I telegraphed for a room at the Poona Club, and, after a breakfast winding up with iced Bombay mangos, the king of fruits, which had been sent up as a present to the Nawab, we left for Hyderabad at nine o'clock, arriving after a hot and very slow journey at 5.20 p.m. At the Secunderabad station, I saw for the first time in my life the beautiful gold mohur-trees in full bloom, and was very much impressed by the sight of an avenue of them. They were one mass of flower, some being of a golden and others of a deep red colour. They are a very favourite tree about here, and are planted at the sides of many of the roads, where they give a brilliant tone to the landscape.

An immense crowd had assembled at Hyderabad station to greet the Nawab on his return home, and as the train drew up they prostrated themselves in front of him, salaaming and taxiring. Here, with regret, we bade good-bye to our hospitable host, and drove off to Dr. Lauder's house, the Nawab, before leaving, having begged the loan of all our trophies to show to the ladies of his zenana, who were, we heard, much interested in the results of our expedition.

I should have much liked to stay again for a few days at Hyderabad, and Dr. and Mrs. Lauder were kind and pressing in their invitations for me to remain, but I was obliged to hurry off to Poona, and Mahableshwar, so I left by the quarter-to-nine train next morning, arriving in due time at Poona, where I had two days hard work before me, packing up and sending to England my purchases, presents, and hunting-trophies, before starting for Mahableshwar, the hill-station seventy miles off, and five thousand feet above the sea, where I was to rejoin their Royal Highnesses the Duke and Duchess of Connaught.

The climate of Poona, I must say, is delightful, and personally I should never wish for cooler weather than one gets there; but of course the hills are more bracing, and so everyone who can get away flies to them at this season of the year. It was now the height of the hot weather, but the club at which I stayed was always pleasant, and I did not require a punkah in my bed-room, as one does in most parts of India; there were no mosquitoes to trouble one at night, and the thermometer never rose above ninety-one degrees in the house, though that meant a good many more degrees in the sun.

I decided to travel by night to Mahableshwar, and hired a tonga and a phaeton; in the former I put my heavy luggage, servant, and monkey, whilst I went in the latter. They had arranged some boards across it on which I laid my bedding and pillows, so that it was far from uncomfortable, and I slept nearly all through the night, waking, however, to see the glorious sun rise in the ghauts.

I was then about thirty miles from Mahableshwar. The road is very steep, and extra horses have to be put on, and even then these poor lean brutes require a great deal of urging and physical arguments to do their work. The scenery is quite lovely. Mountain rises beyond mountain, and one gazes right down into the plain several thousand feet, and sees the cultivation of various crops, whilst higher up is nothing but dense green jungle. The soil is of a bright red colour, and gives a warm glow to the whole scene, whilst the atmosphere is so clear that I could see the sea forty-two miles away.

The trees are covered with orchids, hydrangies, roses, and a beautiful flower both white and yellow, and the gardenia montana grow about the hedgerows. Altogether it was a lovely and refreshing scene, especially to anyone coming up from the hot plains, and I could quite realise now what the hills meant to people who had been struck down by illness, and were ordered there to recruit their health.

About ten miles from Mahableshwar a very pretty village is reached, called Panchganni, which much reminds one of England, with its neat cottages and villas studded about. Here the extra horses are taken off, for the great piece of collar work is over, and here, too, I had some chota hazri at the dâk bungalow before finishing my journey. The rest of my drive was through alternate patches of cultivated land and green jungle, the whole watered by a running stream winding about through grassy banks like an English brook. It is in this district that most of the potatoes consumed in the Bombay Presidency are grown; and two enterprising Chinamen, some years back, had the brilliant idea of starting some market-gardens here, and of growing strawberries. It proved a highly remunerative speculation, and is now one of the features of the place. Small native children ran after the carriage with baskets of strawberries, raspberries, and melons, offering them for a mere trifle.

It is a curious fact that Englishmen, who at home are so fond and proud of their gardens, in India rarely think of cultivating such a thing, and in most districts it is very difficult to get fresh fruit and vegetables. When I was in Hyderabad, I was told that all the best vegetables I saw there came from Ootacamund in the Neilgherry hills; and here, at Mahableshwar, all the pretty little bungalows are surrounded by dense green jungle a few feet from the hall door without the vestige of an attempt to a garden.

The approach to Mahableshwar is lovely. Passing by a lake, the road runs through a shade of thick evergreens, through which are seen peeps of the blue mountains, with their abrupt, precipitous flanks.

At the entrance to the town, I was met by my friend Colonel Rawlins, who came to tell me that the Duke of Connaught had no room for me in his house, and that instead of going into a tent he asked me to come to his bungalow. This was a very kind offer, which I eagerly accepted; and soon afterwards I found myself most comfortably installed in Woodlawn, which is built on the side of a hill, with the jungle for a foreground, whilst over the tree-tops the eye gazes on range after range of blue mountains.

Everything looked so fresh and green. The jungle-fowl were calling in the thick undergrowth close by, the Mahableshwar bulbuls, those beautiful little grey birds with red cheeks and crests, were hopping all about the place; the breakfast-table was laden with lovely melons, figs, strawberries, and mangos, whilst the verandah was a mass of convolvulus creeper in full bloom. I had the kindest of hosts and hostesses; so that, altogether, the scene was quite enchanting, and made one feel that life was worth living.

CHAPTER XIV.

HILL STATIONS—RAINFALL—MAHABLESHWAR—FLOWERS—GENERAL LODWICK — CLUB —AMUSEMENTS — JUNGLE — GAME—WOLVES — TIGER SHOOTING—PICNIC AT WARA—FORT OF PRATAPGHARH—ACCOUNT OF ALZAL KHAN'S MURDER BY SHIVAZI—HEADS OF ENEMY BURIED UNDER TOWERS IN INDIA—WILD BOAR—DUKE OF CONNAUGHT'S LEAVE—OLD LAW, AND REASON WHY—LEAVE MAHABLESHWAR—STRIKE OF COACH PROPRIETORS—WAI—BIG BANIAN-TREE AT WAI-RALGHATH—LEAVE POONA FOR BOMBAY—EMBARK ON PENINSULAR AND ORIENTAL STEAMER 'SUTLEJ'—MONSOON—'JUMNA' TROOPSHIP—WRECK OF 'TASMANIA'—ARRIVE IN ENGLAND.

CHAPTER XIV.

The life is pretty much the same at all the hill-stations of India, and it is a very pleasant change after some months in the plains. Everyone puts business aside for a time, and gives himself up to pleasure; the younger members of society to dancing, tennis, and other amusements, whilst the older and hard-worked officials go in for a thorough rest of mind and body.

As in all small societies made up of idle folk, a great deal of gossip is spread, and for want of better occupation people are interested in the slightest trifles concerning their neighbours. Mahableshwar is in no way free from this foible; but, being the head-quarters of the Governor and Commander-in-Chief of Bombay during the hot season, society is a little more sacred, and is, therefore, not such a hot bed of cancans and gossip as the smaller hill stations.

The rainfall at Mahableshwar is so great that few people remain after the bursting of the monsoon in June, when the whole place is enveloped in thick mists and the roads to the plain are almost impassable. The bungalows are then covered with taties and other contrivances to keep out the wet and damp. All pot-plants are sent off to places in the neighbourhood, especially to Panchganni, where the climate is more genial, and where many English take up their abode during the rains.

The orchids and lilies growing wild in the surrounding jungle are perfectly lovely, and are brought in by the natives in great quantities, and sold for a few annas, forming charming decorations for the dinner-table; and to one fresh from England, where such things are so costly and precious, it seems incredible that so many lovely flowers should be so little thought of. There are said to be thirty distinct kinds of ferns growing in the hills around.

General Lodwick was the first discoverer of Mahableshwar as a fine hill station, and he had it turned to account as a sanatorium. It was in 1824 that he was quartered at Satara, when he undertook the difficult and dangerous task of walking alone and unarmed through the dense jungle to Mahableshwar. He got through it safely, but his dog was killed by a panther on the second day. Lodwick Point, a fine spur of the hills near the town, is named after him, and a monument has been erected to his memory.

A most magnificent view is to be got from this spot, as indeed from almost any part of Mahableshwar when it is not enveloped in the dense mists. These, however, clear away as suddenly as they come.

As usual, in most Indian towns which are the head-quarters of English society, there is a good club, where, as at London clubs, ladies are admitted. Tuesday was the fashionable night, and then the dining-room was always gay, filled as it was with a cheery party of members and their lady friends, who afterwards adjourned to a dance in the big reading-room, the music being supplied by the Governor's excellent band. As I write, I look back to many a pleasant evening spent at the Mahableshwar Club, and from this my experience of an Indian hill station I am inclined to think that the man should consider himself happy whose lines take him to so pleasant a place.

There are a polo ground and numerous tennis courts, where I have witnessed many an exciting match, whilst the little race-meetings, though generally a benefit for one or two particular sportsmen, were always more or less exciting. When one adds to this list picnics, dinners, theatricals, strawberry-parties, &c., it will be seen that life in Mahableshwar passes pleasantly enough.

The jungle all round the station is full of game both big and small, but the foliage is so thick that it is almost impossible to get at or to see any of the animals; that they are there is amply testified by the pud marks of tiger, panther, and deer of all kinds, to say nothing of the depredations committed every now and then on man and beast by the former of these dangerous animals. As usual, however, the natives are apathetic about it, and take no steps to protect themselves.

One day when I was walking out with the Duke of Connaught near Bombay Point, and close to Government House, we saw six wolves in the road about thirty yards in front of us; they looked at us for a few seconds, and then vanished into the jungle.

Tigers abound and do a lot of damage. There is a well-known man-eating tigress about, for which a government reward of one hundred rupees has been offered; but, although she has been 'wanted' now for some years, she has as yet always successfully evaded the numerous shikari who have been after her. We did our best to bag her whilst there, but without success; for, although she killed the beasts we tied up, she never lay up near the dead carcase.

I went out one day, with a large party of friends, to a piece of jungle near Elphinstone Point, and we were very sanguine of success, as she had killed the bail and eaten a great part of it. We were all placed in trees, with comfortable machans rigged up for us, but, when there, we could not see more than half-a-dozen yards around, so that the animal might have easily slipped past between two guns unnoticed. On the second occasion of a kill, I did not go out, and this time the tigress came under Colonel Rawlins's tree. He, unfortunately, was only armed with a Winchester repeating rifle; and, although he fired two shots, and is confident that he hit her, she was never seen again.

Altogether, the shooting at Mahableshwar was not satisfactory, but it served very well as an excuse for a pleasant outing, combined with exercise, and that of a severe kind, as I never came across harder walking in my life.

About this time a tiger was found in the Karli caves, near Poona, and wounded by a man who, unfortunately, was so mauled by the infuriated animal that he died a few days afterwards. It is awful to read of the number of deaths each year in India from wounded tigers and panthers; but of the two the latter inflict by far the most dangerous injuries, for, not being such clean feeders as tigers, their claws are often impregnated with decomposed matter, which gets into the wounds, and produces blood poisoning. There is no doubt that the dangerous part of tiger shooting is following up a beast that has been hit; and this should never be undertaken alone, but by two or three steady shots walking in line armed with heavy rifles. The tiger is naturally a great coward, and will rarely face a resolute body of men, unless wounded.

Lord and Lady Reay contribute a great deal towards the gaieties of Mahableshwar, by giving dinners, dances, and theatricals at Government House; and whilst I was there the Gaekwar of

T 2

Baroda entertained all the residents at an afternoon fête with theatricals in the open, followed by a magnificent display of fireworks after dark. Another time we all went to a picnic at Wara, given by Mr. Crow, the well-known judge. Wara is about eleven miles off. It is a lovely drive right down the ghauts, and lies two thousand feet below Mahableshwar; so that the change of temperature is most distinctly felt in descending. The party included about thirty persons, besides the Duke and Duchess of Connaught.

Near Wara, on one of the spurs of the ghauts, stands the ruins of the old Mahratta fort of Pratapgharh, which played so important a rôle in their history. Most of the party paid it a visit. The ladies were carried by coolies in chairs, whilst the men scrambled up the steep path. Their return in the dark, as seen from Wara, was most picturesque, the numerous coolies carrying lighted torches; so that the whole hill-side was studded with lights gradually descending into the plain.

The fort of Pratapgharh is situated about eight hundred feet above this plain, and is almost inaccessible, except in one spot. It contains two temples, and tanks for collecting water. The old tower is shown under which the head of Alzal Khan, the Bijapur general, was buried in 1659 by Shivaji, who murdered him, and by this treacherous means greatly increased his power. As the story is interesting, and, I think, not much known, I will here relate it.

Alzal Khan was sent with an army from the neighbouring state of Bijapur to take the fort of Pratapgharh and destroy the power of Shivaji. The approach to the place being difficult, Alzal Khan left his army at some distance, and, with a numerous suite, advanced as an envoy to to Shivaji. He was received by the latter in durbar with great civility, and afterwards returned to his camp; but, in the middle of the night, Shivaji, disguised as a Brahmin, visited Pantoji Gopinath, Alzal Khan's chief lieutenant, also a Brahmin, and, addressing him as his superior:

promised money, protection, and the village of Hewra to him and his heirs in perpetuity if he would betray Alzal Khan into his hands.

Pantoji yielded to the bribe and swore fidelity to Shivaji. They now consulted as to the best means of putting their plan into operation, and Pantoji suggested asking Alzal Khan to a conference. Shivaji, therefore, sent for Krishnaji Bhaskar, his vakel, who was also a Brahmin, and to whom he confided the plot, and ordered him, with Pantoji Gopinath, to Alzal Khan's camp, when they told the latter that Shivaji was in great fear of the Bijapur army, and that, if Alzal Khan would give him personal assurance of his life being spared, he might be induced to give himself up.

Alzal Khan fell at once into the trap and agreed to send his army to Jaoli, a matter of some difficulty on account of the nature of the country, whilst he would meet Shivaji below the fort of Pratapgharh.

A road was now cleared for the Khan, but

every other approach was carefully guarded. Shivaji ordered up all his available army under his two generals, Moro and Nestaji Palkar. The latter, with several thousand men, he hid in the jungle near the fort, whilst the picked men, under Moro Trimnial, were sent to the vicinity of the Bijapur army at Jaoli. It was agreed that the signal for Nestaji to attack should be the blast of a horn, whilst Moro, on hearing five guns fired from the Pratapgharh, was to commence his attack.

Alzal Khan approached with fifteen hundred men, but was told by Pantoji Gopinath that such a large body might alarm Shivaji and prevent his coming out of the fort, so he consented to halt them some few hundred yards away, and to himself approach, attended by but one armed follower, whilst he only carried a sword.

Shivaji placed a chain cap under his lungi, chain armour under his cotton gown, and concealed in his hands a most fearful weapon called a waghnakh, of which I have seen a facsimile. It is fixed by rings round the fingers, whilst under the palm it consists of four, sharp knife-blades, bent inwards with a circular twist, so that the hand can be closed and nothing shows but the rings outside. With this instrument in his left hand and a dagger concealed in his dress, he left the fort for the interview.

Alzal Khan had already been some time at the rendezvous, and was getting impatient at the delay, when he saw Shivaji approaching, but halting every now and then as if fearing to advance.

By way of reassuring him, Alzul sent his armed attendant to some distance, though he allowed Shivaji to be closely followed by his two armed men. Alzul Khan now advanced, and they embraced in the usual Oriental fashion; but, whilst so doing, Shivaji struck at his enemy with the waghnakh concealed in his left hand, and ripped him open; at the same time, drawing a dagger out of his clothes with his right hand, he plunged it into his side.

Alzar Khan, having for a moment freed himself from his enemy, struck at him with his sword, but without effect, on account of the chain armour, and before his attendant could come to his assistance he reeled over and died. Said Banden, the attendant, refused to surrender, and was killed. Shivaji's men then cut off Alzal Khan's head, and carried it to the fort, where it was buried and a tower built over it.

In the meanwhile, the signals having been given, Moro rushed upon the Bijapur army and soon caused it to surrender, and by Shivaji's orders spared the lives of all who gave themselves up. Nestaji, however, gave no quarter, and slew the fifteen thousand men round the fort. Shivaji by this stroke took four thousand horses and a number of elephants and cattle, besides an immense amount of treasure, all of which added greatly to his prestige, such ruses being considered quite fair play in the East. Indian history alone furnishes many such examples of treachery and cruelty. The custom of building a tower over the head of an enemy is also common in Indian history. One of the best-known of such cases is that of the Kootab Minar tower near Delhi, which was built by the Emperor of Delhi Kootab aden Altanish, over the head of Prithi raj Shokan, the last Rajpoot King of Delhi.

On our way to the picnic that day we came across a huge wild boar standing in the road before us. The driver of our tonga for a moment did not quite relish his position, thinking that the pig would probably attack the horses; but of that the boar evidently had no intention, for he stepped quietly aside at our approach, and disappeared in the jungle.

Altogether I spent a very pleasant month at Mahableshwar, and was sorry when the time approached for leaving. The Duke and Duchess of Connaught were anxious to be back for the Queen's Jubilee, and had engaged passages in the Peninsular and Oriental steamer *Sutlej*, leaving Bombay on the 24th of May. This was the latest date on which we could possibly start to be in time for the functions in London, but the House of Commons were so long in passing the bill granting the Duke leave that at one time it looked very much as if he would not get away.

By an old law, no commander-in-chief in India can quit the country during the period of his command without resigning office. This was no doubt a very necessary rule in the days when a journey to India occupied six months, in which case an officer might pass a greater part of the time of his command on the high seas; but, now that the journey only takes seventeen or eighteen days, this law might well be rescinded. It would actually be a benefit to the service that the commanders-in-chief should go home and exchange ideas at head-quarters, for during the rains there are no drills, and it is a period of almost enforced idleness.

At last the telegram came announcing that three months' leave had been granted. We left

Mahableshwar early in the morning of the 21st of May. There had been a great stir amongst the coach proprietors, on account of a recent order, issued by the Bombay government, to the police, urging them to use more zeal in prevention of cruelty to the horses on this hilly road. The consequences of this order were twofold, the police detained several horses they did not consider fit to work, and the Parsees, who were the owners, struck work, and would run no more carriages to Poona. We had, however, made a contract some days previously: so they were obliged to take us, or stand an action for breach of contract. As it was, we did not drive directly to Poona, but joined the railway at Wathai, passing through the town of Wai, a very sacred and picturesque place, with many temples and bathing ghats, about eight miles from which, at Wairalgarh, is a famous banian-tree, which, they say, shades three-quarters of an acre of ground with its wide-spreading branches. The road near Wai is planted on each side with fine mango-trees, which at the time I write of were laden with fruit. We reached Wathai at twelve, but then had to wait over three hours for our train, which was very late, and we did not arrive at Poona till eight o'clock.

The next two days were very busy ones, for there was a great deal of packing to be done, many bills to be settled, and good-byes to be said.

We left Poona for Bombay by the eleven p.m. train on the 23rd. A large crowd of friends came to the station to see the party off; and Their Royal Highnesses steamed out amidst ringing cheers, and numerous expressions of regret at their departure, and wishes for a prosperous voyage and speedy return. Having got the luggage and live-stock, and a supply of mangos for friends in England, on board, we left Bombay in the Peninsular and Oriental steamer *Sutlej* at five p.m. next day, and had a very hot journey through the Indian Ocean and Red Sea. The monsoon had just broken, and for three or four days there was a nasty swell on. This entailed closing the ports, which, in such heat, was not pleasant; but the ship was comfortable. There was a cheery party on board, and the whole ship's company, from the captain downwards, was courteous and kind; so that I think nearly everyone really enjoyed the voyage. It seemed almost like a pleasant yachting trip.

At Suez we came up to the *Jumna* troopship, which had left Bombay four days before us, but had broken down in her engines, and consequently lost some time patching them up at Aden. She was full of troops invalided home from Burmah, and these poor fellows had suffered dreadfully from the heat, several of them having died since they left India.

On the morning of the 9th of June we passed close to the wreck of the Peninsular and Oriental steamer *Tasmania* in the Straits of Bonifacio.

The sea was as calm as a lake, so we steamed close up to her, and saw the divers at work. It was a melancholy sight, this beautiful ship, now reduced to a perfect wreck, with only a part of her hull, the top of the funnel, and the masts out of water.

No incident worthy of note occurred during our journey home. We reached Marseilles on the morning of the 10th of June, and, leaving that town by the mail train the same evening, arrived at Charing Cross at a quarter to six p.m., on June 11th, 1887.

THE END